WHAT IS
MY DOG
REALLY
THINKING?

ALLSORTED.
for all your gift books and gift stationery

This edition first published in Great Britain in 2023
by Allsorted Ltd, UK WD19 4BG

© Susanna Geoghegan Gift Publishing

Author: Michael Powell
Editor: Sasha Morton

Photographs under licence from Shutterstock.com

Cover and concept design: Milestone Creative
Contents design: seagulls .net

ISBN: 9781912295913

Printed in China

10 9 8 7 6 5 4 3 2 1

Why does watching a dog be a dog fill one with happiness?

JONATHAN SAFRAN FOER

CONTENTS

INTRODUCTION

Dogs, those loyal, lovable, playful, protective, dopey creatures that share our lives. They sure are puzzling. They can follow our gaze, understand dozens of words and possess an almost mystic ability to emphasize with their human carers and yet they love nothing better than doing zoomies and rolling in badger poo.

Have you ever found yourself staring lovingly at your dog, wondering what mysteries lie behind those trusting eyes? If so, you're not alone. Welcome to the compelling world of canine cognition, where we embark on a quest to unravel the enigma of our beloved companions.

This book is an exploration of the canine psyche, peering into the depths of their thoughts, emotions and desires. It will help you to understand the inner workings of these amazing creatures and sheds light on many of their often-baffling behaviours.

With a blend of scientific research, expert advice and a reader-friendly format, we strive to bridge the communication gap between humans and dogs, to decipher the meaning behind their vocalizations and interpret their often highly nuanced body language.

By understanding what truly goes on inside those noble heads, you can forge a stronger bond with your furry companions. You will gain a deeper appreciation for their perspectives and forever change the way you see your unique canine friends, ensuring they are healthy, happy, and above all, able to express their true selves.

This book follows the conventionally accepted theory that dogs behave similarly to wolves, forming stable family units, or packs. There are other, competing, recent theories that do not accept this is the case; some studies show that feral dogs form looser group associations, so dogs will swap, re-group or change group size regularly. With a mutual ancestor, in so many ways we can see that a dog's behaviour echoes that of wolves, the pack instinct being just one example of this.

WELCOME
HOME

HOW DOES YOUR DOG REACT WHEN YOU ARRIVE HOME? A HAPPY, WELL-BALANCED DOG WHO ISN'T DEPRESSED OR UNWELL, WILL BE UNDERSTANDABLY EXCITED AND HE WILL SHOW IT. IF HE'S UNTRAINED, HE'LL PROBABLY BE BARKING AT THE DOOR BEFORE YOU'VE EVEN GOT YOUR KEY IN THE LOCK, BECAUSE HE HAS LEARNED TO RECOGNISE YOUR FOOTSTEPS AS WELL AS THE SOUND OF YOUR CAR ENGINE.

Many dog owners find the reception they receive to be a mixture of pleasure and inconvenience. They enjoy seeing their dog's delight, but they don't appreciate being ambushed and jumped on, especially if they're carrying bags of shopping. Having to step over a dog, his blanket and several dog toys (AKA welcome home presents), to the sound of incessant barking, can quickly become an irritation. (Especially when he scampers off with a stolen packet of chocolate croissants in his mouth.) Whether you love this happy chaos, or are at least prepared to tolerate it because it's only a few seconds of every day, you're missing the chance to give your dog a social lesson that provides firm but gentle guidance. Following house rules is important. A training technique called 'golden five minutes' achieves this and can also be effective in reducing any separation anxiety your dog might be feeling.

> 'The word "No!" does not teach a dog what you DO want . . . Trying to train your dog by nagging and telling him "No!" each time he does something wrong rather than reinforcing the things he does right will be exhausting for you and confusing for your dog.'
>
> Danielle Shelbourne

Nigel Reed explains this technique in detail in his book, *The Dog Guardian*. He asserts: 'Every time there is a separation from your dog ... the pack has to reunite and the hierarchy has to be determined again'. His definition of 'separation' even includes trips to the bathroom. 'To maintain your status as decision-maker, withhold from greeting your dog until it calms down and leaves you alone,' by which he means ignoring you completely. This could take as long as the average, which is five minutes (hence the name, 'golden five minutes') or even longer. You should call him only when he is calm, no matter how long this takes. Reed advises: 'Do not go up to your dog; always call them to you. This will ensure a clear, natural order of who instructs whom.'

Reed warns that the dog may try all sorts of distractions to get your attention during this cooling-off period, including but not limited to staring, barking, invading your personal space, nudging, leaning against you, pawing, jumping up, bringing you toys and following you around. It is imperative that you give him zero attention, which includes verbal admonishment.

Even negative attention is better than none, so your dog will settle for scolding over silence or being ignored. If he jumps up on the couch and you tell him to get down, he has won because that counts as an interaction. If he jumps up on you, push him down firmly but gently, without looking at him and without reacting emotionally (no laughter, no smiling, no anger, etc.). If he persists with his attention-seeking actions, remove him to another room on his own and close the door. Once he is calm and has left you alone, you can call him to you and give him lots of cuddles, fuss and play. Now he is allowed to express his excitement but on your terms.

Ignoring your dog may feel rude and cruel, but Reed encourages us to think instead of being a 'decision-maker, teaching the dog manners about personal space in a language he understands'. Don't forget that dogs in the wild employ this same method – the pack leader decides the manner, time and place of interaction.

Withdrawing your attention is a powerful training tool that can correct nearly all attention-seeking negative behaviour. When performed correctly, consistently and completely (i.e., don't cave in if it doesn't work immediately), your dog will quickly learn that he only gets the attention he craves when he merits it. He's not stupid. He won't persist with undesirable behaviour if it doesn't get the desired result – your undivided attention.

THERE'S SOMEONE AT THE
DOOR

THE NEXT TIME YOUR DOG RESPONDS TO A KNOCK AT THE DOOR (USUALLY WITH A CONTINUOUS RAPID BARKING WHICH SIGNALS ALERT), PRAISE HIM (YOU SHOULD ALWAYS PRAISE YOUR DOG FOR BEING A GOOD ANTI-PERSONNEL ALARM) AND THEN SPARE A THOUGHT FOR THE THOUSANDS OF YEARS OF WHAT SCIENTISTS CALL 'CO-OPERATIVE EVOLUTION' (GROUPS OF ORGANISMS WORKING OR ACTING TOGETHER FOR COMMON OR MUTUAL BENEFITS) THAT HAVE CULMINATED IN THIS PRECISE MOMENT IN TIME – YOUR DOG DUTIFULLY WARNING YOU ABOUT A POSSIBLE ATTACK BY WILD ANIMALS OR A HOSTILE TRIBE.

> 'Dogs teach us a very important lesson in life: The mailman is not to be trusted.'
>
> Sian Ford

A quick internet search reveals lots of articles online offering advice on how to stop your dog from barking at the front door. One typical example, published on wagwalking.com, claims: 'There is nothing worse than having to listen to your pup bark his head off and go crazy every time someone knocks on your door or rings the bell. Not only is the noise annoying, it is very rude behaviour and might scare off the visitor.' Yet the very next line acknowledges that this is 'a very natural behaviour for your dogs'.

Why fight thousands of years of co-operative evolution? A dog's ability to tolerate humans and to pay attention to us has enabled a hard-wired channel of communication to grow between our two species. These unique social skills have made dogs invaluable as companions, hunters and protectors and have allowed us to co-evolve over millennia.

> 'Evolution is not any different to gravity. If I drop a ball, I can't stop it from dropping; it's unstoppable force. Evolution is also unstoppable. Just because you can't see, it does not mean it's not acting all the time.'
>
> Research scientist and dog expert, Vanessa Woods

Our direct ancestors are precisely those ancient humans who were predisposed to coexist with dogs and benefit from barked warnings when strangers approached; they would also have hunted more effectively.

OK, you can stand down from high alert now – it was just Deliveroo at the door! But what your dog just did – barking to tell you that there was someone outside – is no less remarkable a feat than being able to order a burger at 4am. Incidentally, if your dog continues to bark even after the stranger has walked away again, it's probably because you haven't acknowledged that you have heard and appreciated his warning. Give him some praise. Rub his ears and tell him he's a really good barker! This acknowledgment is not only pleasurable for the dog, it gives him a clear signal that he too can step down from high alert. Aha! You hadn't considered that, had you?

> 'Saying thank you when your dog barks shows it that the role of alerting you to potential dangers to the pack is vital. By getting up and looking at the problem, you are showing it that you are dealing with the issue.'
>
> Nigel Reed, *The Dog Guardian*

All too often, we ignore our dogs' attempts to communicate, which must be very frustrating and increase their anxiety levels. It is self-evident to you that answering the door resolves the issue of who is at the door and why, but your dog always needs your feedback and this will stop him from nuisance barking after the visitor has long gone.

It is important to calmly acknowledge your dog every time he barks at a perceived danger, not just when the doorbell rings: 'It does not matter where the perceived danger comes from, be it in the garden or at the window, dogs on the television or in the park, thunder and lightning ... your dog will need your acknowledgement and calm reaction to understand that you are dealing with the problem,' says Nigel Reed.

If you respond to his barking by shouting at him to be quiet, you send him two negative messages: the first is that he doesn't matter and the second is that you are agitated, so naturally, he responds with increased agitation and more barking because you just raised the perceived danger level. Congratulations: you just created a vicious circle.

PLAY
WITH ME

WHEN DOGS WANT TO PLAY, THEY USE SPECIFIC
BODY LANGUAGE AND BEHAVIOURS TO
COMMUNICATE THIS TO OTHER DOGS, OR THEIR OWN
HUMAN COMPANIONS. THE MOST WELL-KNOWN
DOGGY INVITATION TO PLAY IS THE PLAY BOW:
WHEN THE DOG CROUCHES TO FACE HER PLAYMATE
WITH HER FRONT LEGS EXTENDED FLAT ON THE
GROUND AND HER BACKSIDE IN THE AIR.

The first game on the agenda is usually 'chase me', so often the play bow is followed by a quick dash away from, or towards, the playmate. A play bow will often be accompanied by several other obvious gestures – tail wagging in a very loose manner, or a big circle, barking with excitement, bringing you toys, jumping up at you – or doing 'zoomies'. Zoomies are those moments whe a dog starts running around in circles or running and leaping back and forth energetically and with an exaggerated gait. However, even though these behaviours are the universal dog language for 'play with me', some dogs have other unique ways of indicating that they want to play, so be attentive to your own dog's subtle invitations.

If an initial play bow doesn't give the other dog sufficient reassurance to join in, especially when a big adult dog is gently enticing a reticent puppy, you'll often see the more dominant dog roll on its back, which signals apparent submission.

Play is vital for dogs because it allows them to develop coordination, learn their social position within a pack, rehearse situations such as escaping from danger, self-defence and hunting and most important of all, learn how to roughhouse without overstepping the boundaries of safety or friendliness. But there is a further dimension. Stanley Coren, author of *How to Speak Dog*, explains: 'In most animals, playfulness begins to disappear as the individuals become adults. However, human beings have bred dogs to keep ... the lifelong desire to play. This is important for people, because we humans also retain our childhood curiosity and playfulness throughout our whole lives.'

Sometimes it can be hard to tell the difference between play and genuine aggression, because some of the body language is the same. Pinned ears, an erect tail, growling and showing teeth, barging and wrestling can mean 'I'm not happy' and also 'Play with me!' – which is why dogs intersperse a sophisticated repertoire of deflection signals – sniffing, yawning, sneezing, scratching and licking – to diffuse tension. These signal that all is well and that this is still a game, no matter how rough it might appear. Also, the play bow remains the most important signal throughout the game; dogs use it frequently during play to remind everyone that 'We're still all friends here!'

'Given the importance of regular visual assurances that the game is still a game', says Alexandra Horowitz, author of *Inside of a Dog*, 'it is perhaps not surprising that successful three-way rough-and-tumble play is much rarer than play between two dogs ... typically, only dogs familiar with each other pull off threesomes.'

DID YOU KNOW?

Familiar dogs will often abbreviate the play bow into a 'play slap' – front legs slapping the ground together at the beginning of the bow.

THAT'S MINE,
GET OFF

WHEN YOUR DOG GUARDS HER TOYS OR GETS
PROTECTIVE ABOUT HER FOOD, SHE WILL USUALLY
EMIT A LOW-PITCHED GROWL, WHILST STARING
FIXEDLY AT WHATEVER IT IS THAT SHE IS CLAIMING
AS HER OWN. ALTERNATIVELY, SHE MIGHT FREEZE,
KEEPING HER HEAD SIDEWAYS TO YOU, AND TURN HER
EYES TOWARDS YOU AS SHE GROWLS, SO THAT YOU
CAN SEE THE WHITES OF HER EYES.

The growl shows that she means business and most owners find it deeply worrying that their dog should be issuing warnings at such a high intensity of threat. Isn't the owner supposed to be in charge? Yes, and while resource guarding (RG) is normal behaviour, you should be able to approach your dog while she is playing or eating without fear of being attacked.

'Guarding toys is a completely normal behaviour for dogs and punishing them for it is like punishing a child for being protective of their favourite toy.'

Nicole Ellis, expert dog trainer

So why does she insist on guarding her things? Applied animal behaviourist, Patricia McConnell, who has been working with, studying and writing about dogs for over

twenty-five years explores this in her online blog, 'The Other End of the Leash'. She says: 'That's easy to answer: We don't know. Seriously, we really, really don't know. Does growing up in a large litter and having to fight for food make a difference? Could there be a genetic predisposition to resource guarding?' She could find no information so she emailed a list of Certified Applied Animal Behaviourists to ask if there was any research on genetic or environmental factors related to RG. She concluded that, 'There simply doesn't appear to be anything out there on this specific topic'. Although she is willing to assert that there is a strong genetic component, but she also cites her own experience of working 'with litters of 11 dogs in which the biggest and strongest (and first to get to the nipple) pup became the RG dog very early in life'.

Regardless of how this resource-guarding behaviour has developed in dogs as a species, it's safe to say that anxiety is undoubtedly a strong factor. Like humans, dogs may experience anxiety when they sense that something they hold dear might be removed from their possession. When you approach, this increases her anxiety. Rightly or wrongly, she thinks that you are going to remove something from her.

It is important that you don't punish her for guarding her possessions as this will have the opposite effect to what you want. If the fear of losing valuable possessions is her primary motive for guarding, then punishing or reprimanding her and/or removing the items in question inevitably leads to heightened distress, causing her to double down on her guarding next time.

So you need to teach her two things: firstly, that on the whole, you have no desire to take her things; they are safe, and secondly,that even if you did happen to briefly remove one of her toys, she could have it back again or something else in return. This desensitises her to the importance of guarding her stuff, so that she learns to trust that even should you take something, it's not gone forever and that you will soon return it to her.

Play a swapping game to put this into action. Gather a bunch of her favourite squeaky toys and some food treats. Offer her one of them. As she tries to grab it, quickly whisk the one she's guarding away from her. She may be too focused on her new spoils to worry about the first toy, but if she does make a fuss, give it back to her. In this way, she gets to make the choice and she wins every time. She learns that she can have her toy and another one.

In fact, you are both winning because you are teaching her to feel safe around you and her possessions and she gets to have lots of fun snatching toys off you and choosing which ones she wants to play with. Not only is it heaps of fun, it's empowering for her, even though you maintain ultimate control by defining the parameters of the game.

THAT'S FUNNY

EVERYONE AGREES THAT DOGS WAG THEIR TAILS
WHEN THEY'RE HAPPY (AND ALSO IN OTHER
CIRCUMSTANCES) BUT THERE IS LESS CONSENSUS
ABOUT THEIR ABILITY TO SMILE. MOST DOG OWNERS
WILL SWEAR THAT THEIR DOGS SMILE AT THEM.

After all, with their almond-shaped eyes pulled up slightly at the outer corners, mouth slightly open and the tongue sticking forward, lolling over the front teeth, what else could they be doing? Many scientists would readily agree with them. But what about laughter?

Dog 'laughter' appears to have a lot less anecdotal support. Could it be anthropomorphism taken one step too far? Most agree that a dog 'smile' is at the very least what Stanley Coren describes in *Do Dogs Dream?* as, 'A casual expression that is usually seen when the dog is relaxed, playing or interacting socially (especially with people). The moment any anxiety or stress is introduced into the situation, the dog's mouth closes and you can no longer see the tongue'.

He also points out that this facial expression has 'been recognised for a long time as representing a smile'. He cites the discovery of children's toys dating back to ancient Egypt, including a dog on wheels designed to be pulled along the floor by a string. He says that the translation of the name of the toy is 'the smiling dog' and that its face 'has an exaggerated large tongue lapping out over his front teeth'.

So, if there was any debate about a dog's ability to smile, it seems that the ancient Egyptians resolved the question thousands of years ago. From an evolutionary perspective, having a smiley expression has a selective advantage, because a smiley dog is more appealing to its human breeders. Therefore, it's little wonder that this trait has been passed on and probably become even more pronounced.

Until recently, the existence of laughter in the animal kingdom was less established. Animal behaviourists used to believe that laughter was the sole preserve of humans and apes (Charles Darwin was one of the first to notice that chimpanzees and other great apes produce a laugh-like sound when they are tickled or when they are playing). But recently, researchers at UCLA identified 65 species of animals that make 'play vocalizations' or what we would call laughter. We've known for some time that apes and rats laugh, but there are many others, including lots of primates, domestic cows, dogs, foxes, mongooses, seals and three species of bird (not including parrots and mynah birds – their sounds are just mimicry).

Nobel-Prize-winning ethologist Konrad Lorenz has confirmed that dogs are capable of laughing which he identifies as a kind of panting. In his book, *Man Meets Dog*, Lorenz says: 'An invitation to play always follows; here the slightly opened jaws which reveal the tongue, and the tilted angle of the mouth which stretches almost from ear to ear give a still stronger impression of laughing. This "laughing" is most often seen in dogs playing with an adored master and which become so excited that they soon start panting.'

Patricia Simonet from Sierra Nevada College in Lake Tahoe has recorded the sounds made by dogs playing in parks and observed, 'To an untrained human ear, it sounds much like a pant, "hhuh, hhuh"'. But further study revealed that these laughs could be distinguished from ordinary dog panting by their broader range of frequencies. In another experiment, she played this recorded canine laughter to 15 puppies, who responded joyfully. She has also used the recordings to calm dogs in an animal shelter and they even responded favourably when she attempted to mimic the canine laughter.

Stanley Coren has also practised producing canine laughter. He admits to having been initially 'a bit sceptical about the usefulness of humans making these dog laugh sounds' but after experimenting with his own dogs, he developed a technique which he describes as 'something like "hhuh-hhah-hhuh-hhah …" with the "hhuh" sound made with slightly rounded lips, while the "hhah" sound is made with a sort of open-mouthed smiling expression'.

He describes the resulting 'laugh' as 'breathy with no actual voicing' such that there is no discernible vibration coming from the voice box. He reports that his dogs responded by sitting up, wagging their tails and approaching him from across the room. He has also used his dog laugh successfully in obedience classes to put moderately worried, anxious or shy dogs at their ease.

IS THAT ME?
NAH

BEING ABLE TO RECOGNISE ONESELF IN A MIRROR
COMES NATURALLY TO HUMANS; BETWEEN THE AGES
OF 18 TO 24 MONTHS, A TYPICALLY-DEVELOPING
BABY GAINS THIS ABILITY WITHOUT BEING TAUGHT.
CHIMPANZEES, ORANGUTANS, GORILLAS AND DOLPHINS
ALSO SHOW SELF-AWARENESS WHEN PRESENTED WITH A
MIRROR. BUT WHEN DOGS SEE THEIR OWN REFLECTION,
THEY EITHER THINK THEY ARE LOOKING AT ANOTHER
DOG OR THEY IGNORE IT COMPLETELY.

Dogs demonstrate a range of complex cognitive abilities, which include reading human emotions, understanding human gestures and learning an impressive vocabulary. But because they 'fail' the mirror test, psychologists refuse to accept that their intelligence can extend to one of the most advanced aspects of consciousness: self-awareness. Therefore, the issue still hasn't been satisfactorily resolved.

Some studies have suggested that dogs may possess a limited form of self-awareness. Some argue that it is wrong to place too much emphasis on mirrors and that evidence should be sought instead through a dog's primary sense – smell. In the spirit of the quotation often wrongly attributed to Albert Einstein: 'Everybody is a genius. But if you judge a fish by its ability to climb a tree, it will live its whole life believing that it is stupid.'

Studies have been carried out to test dogs' abilities to recognise their own scent rather than their own reflection. At the University of Colorado, biologist and ethologist Marc Bekoff used his dog Jethro as a test subject over five winters. He reports: 'I walked behind Jethro and scooped up his yellow snow and moved it to different, clean locations some distance down the trail. I also gathered yellow snow from other dogs and moved it.' He monitored Jethro's behaviour and observed that he sniffed more at the urine of other dogs than at his own, suggesting that 'he seemed to recognise his own scent'.

Bekoff's tireless research suggests that dogs are capable of complex cognitive processes, such as understanding cause and effect, problem-solving, and learning through observation. In his book, *The Emotional Lives of Animals*, he argues that dogs have emotions and personalities that are unique to them, and that they can experience a wide range of emotions, including joy, fear, anger, and love. He argues that dogs do share some aspects of self-awareness with humans, including a sense of having a body, with body parts that belong to them. They also have a sense of what belongs to them beyond their own bodies, including territory, objects and food. But he failed to establish whether dogs have made that huge intellectual leap of having a sense of 'me-ness' that is in any way equivalent to that of humans and certain primates and dolphins.

> 'When we allow ourselves to see beyond what our mind tells us is there, we start to tap into the vastness of consciousness that lies within us and within all living beings.'
>
> Marc Bekoff

Overall, the question of whether dogs have self-awareness remains a topic of ongoing scientific inquiry. Bekoff would no doubt argue that our priority should be to move beyond grading animals intellectually. Instead, we should focus instead on creating a world in which we finally recognise that the rights of every living creature are as sacred as our own.

WHAT'S THAT SMELL?

WHEN YOU TAKE YOUR DOG FOR A WALK AND SHE INSISTS ON STOPPING EVERY FEW YARDS TO CATCH THE SCENTS OF OTHER DOGS, HER BRAIN IS HIGHLY STIMULATED. SHE IS NOT ONLY THINKING, BUT SHE IS ALSO ANALYSING AND INTERPRETING THE IMPORTANT INFORMATION THAT SHE IS PICKING UP THROUGH HER NOSE.

Your dog's sense of smell is her dominant sense; it is her primary method of understanding her surroundings, not only for hunting prey (not so important now that she has you to feed her), but to collect the social messages that other dogs leave behind in their urine. Dog expert, Stanley Coren explains: 'In many ways, the canine equivalent of ink is urine. Many of the chemicals that give information about a dog's age, sex, emotional state, sexual availability, and health are found dissolved in its urine.' So, when your dog is rooting around a lamppost or a dubious sticky patch on the pavement, be patient. Don't pull her away. This is the single most important mental stimulation a dog can receive during a walk. Not only does it keep her up to date with all the comings and goings of other dogs in the neighbourhood, but her brain also is fizzing and firing on all cylinders, sifting and storing information. It's a cognitive workout. Brain gym.

31

Dogs need this regular brain mental and olfactory stimulation to stay healthy and mentally fit. Imagine if your only source of news was reading scraps of paper lying around in the road, or hearing snippets of radio coming from a speaker embedded in every other lamp post.

Not only would your brain crave this input, but you'd also quickly become frustrated if you spotted a juicy headline, or someone's photograph, only to be suddenly yanked away by your impatient owner. There's nothing wrong with your dog interpreting the scent messages of other dogs. Don't deprive your dog of gleaning all the gossip on the street. If your dog sniffing urine makes you feel queasy, think of it instead as doggie social media.

All dogs have special sweat glands called 'apocrine glands' which secrete the pheromones which carry vital personal information. These glands are spread over the entire body but are most concentrated in the genital and anal areas. Humans also have apocrine glands in certain areas of the body, although the groin and armpits have the greatest concentration. That's why your dog often shows particular interest in your crotch area. This makes most dog owners uncomfortable, but it is natural canine behaviour. If you want it to stop, distract your dog with something more interesting rather than scold her.

I LOVE YOU

DOGS SHOW THEIR AFFECTION FOR US WITH A VARIETY OF BEHAVIOURS. SOME ARE WELL-KNOWN – TAIL WAGGING, LICKING, CUDDLING AND BURSTING WITH EXCITEMENT WHEN YOU RETURN HOME – BUT OTHERS ARE MORE SUBTLE. REST ASSURED THAT DOGGY LOVE ISN'T HUMAN PROJECTION, IT'S BACKED UP BY SCIENCE. *HOW DO I LOVE THEE? LET ME COUNT THE WAYS.*

Fortunately, several science experiments have studied this very subject. Scientists at Emory University found that when dogs and their owners gaze into each other's eyes, both the dogs and the owners experience an increase in the hormone oxytocin. Oxytocin is secreted by the posterior lobe of the pituitary gland, a pea-sized structure at the base of both brains, which makes you both feel good and deepens your social bond. So, if you and your dog love staring at one another, keep it up, it's good for both of you! But don't stare at stranger dogs, who will interpret this as a direct challenge.

Dogs use licking socially for several reasons: to show affection, express submission and seek attention. Sometimes licking has no other purpose than to express affection, but it also helps to generate a common pack smell. Your arm ends up smelling of dog drool while he gets to explore your taste and scent. It's a win-win! If your dog steals your best sweater, it's only because he can't get enough of your comforting odour – chewing and snuggling with it makes him feel safe and secure.

Licking for grooming and cleaning is also an important way of displaying affection and deepening bonds. He may also lick to comfort you when you're feeling sad or anxious – because he cares about you. A study published in the journal *Animal Cognition* found that dogs were more likely to approach a crying person than someone who was humming or talking, although they usually responded to weeping by becoming submissive (possibly because of their heightened anxiety).

Following you around the house means he loves spending time with you and mirroring is another indicator of love. For example, if your dog yawns directly after you, it means that you share a close bond. We have unwittingly bred dogs to do this because human beings prefer the company of people who subtly mimic their gestures and body language, and the same applies to our animals.

Studies have shown that dogs will mimic an owner's behaviour for as long as ten minutes after the event. This 'deferred imitation' is a highly sophisticated cognitive skill. 'They do it so naturally because dogs are predisposed to learn socially from us,' explains Ádám Miklósi, a behavioural ethologist at Eötvös Loránd University in Budapest, who has studied this phenomenon extensively.

When you come home,your dog's excitement is an unmistakable display of affection. He wants to jump on you and smother you with a frenzy of licks. However, this is considered to be bad manners amongst dogs as well as humans. Perhaps you've noticed that many dogs self-regulate by fetching a toy, blanket or a personal item like a slipper to present to their owner as a gift? Introducing an element of play into the greeting like this is a common way for dogs to show love whilst diverting their excessive energy to achieve a more socially acceptable outcome.

'Nigel inspires real love … but Nigel has the rare gift of taking our love and making us feel enriched and enlarged by doing so. It is not what he gives back to us so much as what he allows us to give to him.'

Monty Don, talking about his Golden Retriever
in *Nigel: My Family and Other Dogs*

When you enter a room and find your dog lying down, or if you talk to him when you're relaxing together, he may respond with a single, almost perfunctory tail wag. This is his way of checking in with you, expressing his contentment and acknowledging that he still loves you.

Another way you can tell that your dog trusts and loves you is the pleasure that he gets when you give him a good ear rub. By placing your hands on a dog's head, you are asserting your dominance, which is why an unfamiliar dog may not react positively to your uninvited physical attention. Most dogs will only let you mess with their ears after you have formed a close bond.

It's easy to read the pleasure on your dog's face when you tenderly cup his head and run your fingertips behind his ears to deliver a heavenly massage. Your dog might respond by closing his eyes, slightly lifting his chin and even taking deep breaths or snorting in pure bliss. But what makes an ear rub so special for dogs?

The answer is simple: there's a concentrated network of nerve fibres in and around that area (the same is true of the belly and between the toes, two other sensitive areas that dogs usually only allow trusted individuals to rub). Stroking this area stimulates these nerves, as well as the pituitary and hypothalamus glands, which release endorphins into the bloodstream. It also helps to relax the neck muscles to improve blood circulation in that region, and it acts as a natural sedative for both the dog and the owner. Research studies indicate that rubbing a dog's ears can decrease our own blood pressure and promote the release of feel-good chemicals in our bodies.

SORRY,
I CAN'T HEAR YOU
(I CAN REALLY)

POSSIBLY THE MOST FRUSTRATING, INCONVENIENT
AND EMBARRASSING THING A DOG CAN DO (WORSE
THAN ROLLING IN BADGER POO, CHEWING YOUR
POSSESSIONS, HUMPING YOUR GUESTS' LEGS, BEGGING
OR BARKING FOR NO REASON, CARPET SURFING,
LEASH PULLING, SLOBBERING AND SHEDDING
EVERYWHERE) IS REFUSING TO COME WHEN CALLED.

Conversely, a 'solid recall' is possibly the most important thing you must train your dog to do, not only for the sake of your sanity but for your dog's safety and that of other humans and animals. A dog who won't come back when you call is a liability that could get itself and you into deep trouble. Why is it so important? Well, a loose dog presents a multitude of dangers.

Dogs love to be outdoors, but in our modern world, the outdoors isn't very dog-proof. Traffic is clearly one of the biggest dangers, but there are many scenarios where solid recall is imperative. For example, imagine you are walking along a deserted country track, just about wide enough for a rough-terrain vehicle to drive along. Your dog is off leash because the chances of you meeting a vehicle here are slim. But around the next corner could lurk a host of problems – a tractor carrying a ton bale on a spike (the driver has poor visibility); a flock of sheep or cows being herded from one field to another; two horse riders, a huge muddy puddle or a family of cyclists. In each case, the only way you could guarantee everybody's safety would be to call your dog back to you and put her on a leash. Loose dogs also get lost and end up in dog pounds.

Even if you're a staunch urbanite, a local park holds just as many hazards – young children, other dogs, several exits onto busy roads, areas that are out of bounds (e.g., an electricity substation in the corner), a family having a picnic, cyclists, runners, etc.

WHAT IS MY DOG REALLY THINKING?

There is nothing more relaxing than taking your dog somewhere off-leash and knowing with one hundred percent certainty that she will stop whatever she is doing and come back to you when you call her. Clearly, the recall instinct varies hugely between breeds. For example, Golden Retrievers have been bred to bring game back to their owners, so recall is built into their special purpose. But for other breeds, such as scent hounds, once they pick up a scent, you can find yourself calling them for hours to no avail.

In fact, some experts and breeders advise never letting certain breeds off the lead. For example, Otterhounds have a fearsome reputation for not coming back.

> In the world of Otterhounds running off-leash is controversial ... Hours of obedience training are critical. But most of all, we always evaluate the surroundings for access to streets, open fields etc. before we make a decision to let the hounds run free. We just have to be smarter than their scent instinct.
>
> Ashka Gordon, AKC Otterhound Breeders of Merit

There are hosts of websites and books that will tell you how to train your dog to come when called, but in their book, *Outwitting Dogs*, Terry Ryan and Kirsten Mortensen boil it down to two key rules:

- Your dog must know that the rewards for returning to you are better than the rewards for doing anything else.

- You and your dog must practise the come behaviour until his response is a deeply ingrained habit.

You can add a third rule: Never punish your dog if she doesn't respond when you want her to. You don't want her to associate recall and training with being told off. Dogs do and can learn through fear and punishment, but rewards and no-fault learning is the only humane method.

41

Most trainers would recommend using food to teach your dog that paying attention to you is rewarding. They can be anything your dog loves, but small, because you're going to need at least 30 of them each day, plus you don't want to overfeed her. You don't need to use large treats because have you noticed how much time your dog is prepared to spend snuffling along the kitchen floor just to find one grain of rice or a microscopic fragment of cheese?

You can use praise, but dogs have a special relationship with food. A food treat has the added advantage that you can use it when luring to get her attention and position her. You lure your dog by holding a treat over her nose in your closed fist, using the smell to steer her into a position for the first few tries, then transition the luring motion into a hand signal and finally add a verbal cue.

Some people get concerned that having to give your dog food to gain her obedience is a display of weakness, like paying a bribe. Terry Ryan and Kirsten Mortensen have a solid comeback for this: 'A bribe is when you pay someone, up front, to either do something or promise not to do something. When you use food to train a dog, though, you never pay up front. You dispense the food after your dog has completed a behaviour. Yes, your dog will be working for the food, but you've set the criteria.'

I'M A HAPPY
DOG

DOGS AND HUMANS HAVE COEXISTED FOR
THOUSANDS OF YEARS, ALLOWING DOGS
TO DEVELOP FACIAL EXPRESSIONS THAT
RESEMBLE THOSE OF HUMANS. THIS MEANS
UNDERSTANDING A HAPPY DOG'S FACE AND
BODY LANGUAGE IS INSTINCTIVE FOR US.

If your dog appears to be grinning, with an open mouth, a bit of tongue protruding, lips loose or curling upward, she's happy. The face may be wrinkled but it's easy to interpret these happy wrinkles. Happy dogs keep their heads in a neutral position, with no abdominal tucking, arching of the back or tucking down of the backside.

A relaxed facial expression, with eyes rounded and soft with occasional blinks are also common signs of relaxation. She may wag her tail broadly and gently from side to side, and if her happiness tips over into excitement, she'll increase the pace. The ears might be pricked up because she is feeling engaged and expecting good things, or down and relaxed.

In his book, *How to Speak Dog*, Stanley Coren describes what he calls a 'contentment roll' which 'is most often seen after something pleasant has occurred, such as immediately after feeding,' although it can also happen when the dog anticipates something pleasant is coming, such as food. We've all seen our dogs do this: the dog rolls on his back and rubs her shoulders on the ground. This is sometimes preceded by a 'nose rubbing', where 'the dog pushes its face, and possibly its chest, against the ground in a rubbing motion. It can also be associated with an exaggerated rubbing of the dog's face with its forepaw in a direction that goes from eyes to nose. 'Dogs often perform this contentment roll after a burst of excited activity. For example, when you go to the park and let your dog off the lead, she may bounce away from you, full of excess energy, wagging her tail in a broad circle, or she might tear around in circles. Then, once she's run off this initial burst of adrenalin, that's when you'll see her almost faceplant straight into a nose, face and back rub 'n' roll. This expression of pure, unbridled happiness is infectious.

It's self-evident but still worth mentioning that a happy dog is playful and affectionate. A happy dog will wag her tail and be eager to play with toys or other dogs or enjoy a petting and a cuddle. But equally, she might express her contentment and relaxation with signs of sleepiness, such as yawning or dozing off nearby. Unhappy dogs don't sleep, they pace, especially if they are in pain, so if your dog is enjoying a nap, it's usually a good sign (i.e., it's more likely she's happy rather than bored or ill).

The direction of a tail wag is significant. Dogs wag more to the right when they meet a familiar person or dog and more to the left when meeting an unfamiliar dog or face possible conflict.

I TRUST YOU

THE BOND BETWEEN HUMANS AND DOMESTICATED DOGS IS UNPARALLELED IN THE ANIMAL KINGDOM. THIS INCREDIBLE PARTNERSHIP HAS BEEN FLOURISHING FOR OVER 20,000 YEARS, REPRESENTING A REMARKABLE SUCCESS STORY. THROUGHOUT HISTORY, HUMANS HAVE SELECTIVELY BRED DOGS FOR VARIOUS PURPOSES SUCH AS HUNTING, HERDING, PROTECTION, COMPANIONSHIP, LOYALTY AND EMOTIONAL SUPPORT BUT AT THE ROOT OF THESE IS TRUST.

You might remember that at the start of the book, we touched upon a dog's ability to trust humans and to pay attention to us via a hard-wired channel of communication between our two species. (Full marks if you recall that this phenomenon is what scientists call 'co-operative evolution' – groups of organisms working or acting together for their common or mutual benefit.) Dogs, like any other animal, are affected by their past experiences, socialization, and genetics, which can influence their ability to trust humans and other animals. Traumatic experiences, like abuse or neglect, may result in trust issues, fear, or aggression in dogs. Sometimes, even a single traumatic incident can have a long-lasting impact. Establishing trust with a nervous or fearful dog is a gradual process and demands composed and consistent handling.

The key to building trust is to respond to your dog's need for routine and structure. Make your dog feel secure by providing a safe environment with lots of positive interactions and a high degree of routine and predictability. Conversely, many dogs feel uneasy around children because they tend to be more impulsive and unpredictable than adults. (We look at this in more detail towards the end of the book.)

Focus on consistent mealtimes, walks, play, training and socialisation as you build your dog's confidence and trust with humans and other dogs. With most dogs, this happens organically, especially if they are homed during the critical period of puppyhood, which is between three to fourteen weeks of age. Lack of proper socialization at this stage of a puppy's development can result in a dog becoming fearful or aggressive towards people and other animals. Also, certain breeds are genetically more predisposed to friendliness and sociability than others.

Regularly groom and pet your dog to help her develop a positive association with physical contact and learn to trust your touch. A trusting dog will allow you to touch her anywhere, even vulnerable areas such as belly, paws and ears. Her ultimate display of this bond is to lie on her back and show you her belly, which means she feels completely relaxed and trusting in your company. This posture can also indicate submission, as it's a way for dogs to communicate to each other that they are not a threat (see page 89).

It's important to always handle dogs with patience and empathy, especially if they have had a rough start in life. A trusting dog will show a lack of fear and anxiety in your presence and in her surroundings; she will actively seek you out and want to spend time with you.

DID YOU KNOW?

You should avoid towering over an anxious dog; instead, sit on the floor or squat down until you're at her eye level.

I'M FEELING
ANXIOUS

UNTIL QUITE RECENTLY, MANY SCIENTISTS
DISMISSED THE IDEA THAT DOGS EXPERIENCE AN
EMOTIONAL LIFE LIKE HUMANS DO, AND SOME
HAVE EVEN DOUBTED THEIR ABILITY TO FEEL PAIN.
FORTUNATELY, THE CONSENSUS NOW IS THAT DOGS
EXPERIENCE STRESS AND ANXIETY AND THAT THEY
CAN AND DO SUFFER FROM DEPRESSION.

49

WHAT IS MY DOG REALLY THINKING?

First, let's explore the body language that dogs use when something in their immediate environment causes them to experience momentary anxiety, such as a strange dog or a loud noise (e.g. fireworks). The anxiety goes away once its cause has been removed. Typically, the dog will have lips clamped and pulled back or open. The face may become stiff and ridged with tension, with ears up and back. The tail is tucked in between the legs and the backside might curve downwards, with the back legs bent or braced in a distinctive cowering pose.

Also, whereas a happy dog has a smiling mouth and either round moist 'shiny' eyes or soft almond-shaped eyes, anxiety causes the eyes to widen so that the whites (the sclera) become visible. If the dog is looking to the side, the whites will form a half-moon shape. This is known as 'whale-eye' and is a common canine response to a perceived threat – turning her head away from something but keeping her eyes on it. Humans do the same when we don't want to become involved in a potentially dangerous situation by staring directly at it.

50

Another sign of anxiety is the spatulated tongue (wide and cupped to resemble a large spoon) caused by stress-induced panting. This is easily mistaken for a happy tongue or the result of normal panting, but in these circumstances, the tongue is lolling and relaxed and flops downwards over the lower jaw. A spatulated tongue is held upward and more rigidly by muscular tension. It can also be an indicator of overheating, which is a stressful situation. Sometimes the tongue rolls up so much that it can form a cylinder shape as it rests on the front teeth.

Longer-term, habitual anxiety is a more difficult issue, the most common of which is separation anxiety. Symptoms include barking or howling, causing damage, defecating or urinating when left alone, pacing, excessive panting or drooling (a sign of high anxiety) and becoming anxious when anyone prepares to leave the house. Unless your dog has been badly neglected in the past, this is fixable by reducing her time spent alone and by offering her a distraction such as a Kong toy filled with healthy treats to keep her entertained while you're out. Ask your vet for further advice.

There are nine million dogs in the UK alone, and a recent report by a pet insurance company revealed widespread anxiety and depression among domestic pets. Figures show 623,000 dogs and cats in the UK suffer mentally each year, with more than 900,000 suffering a loss of appetite because of stress or emotional problems.

Most dogs can recover quickly from stress-inducing situations, such as fireworks, but when a dog frequently holds tension in its body and displays chronic anxiety – even in the absence of specific triggers – it's often a sign that the dog is suffering from long-term anxiety disorder.

Just like humans, dogs with chronic anxiety get worn out by the constant flood of stress hormones in their bloodstream. When a dog is unable to get away from whatever is causing the stress, or there isn't sufficient time to recover, this can lead to chronic illnesses such as heart and kidney disease, or high blood pressure, as well as interference with learning and memory.

If you suspect that this applies to your dog, then observe her closely and consider three factors of her anxious behaviour: frequency, duration and intensity. If you suspect any of these factors to be abnormally high or that her anxiety is interfering with her daily life and/or yours, seek advice from a veterinarian.

'Nearly all dogs have an increase in stress hormones the moment they are left alone. The severity of their anxiety symptoms will determine the level of intervention and treatment.'

Carling Matejka

I'M VERY AFRAID

IT IS IMPORTANT TO NOTE THAT SOME DOGS MAY EXHIBIT DIFFERENT BEHAVIOURS WHEN THEY ARE AFRAID, AND THAT THESE MAY VARY DEPENDING ON THE INDIVIDUAL DOG AND THEIR PAST EXPERIENCES. THERE'S A LOT OF CROSSOVERS BETWEEN EXTREME FEAR AND THE ANXIETY SIGNALS DISPLAYED IN THE PREVIOUS CHAPTER SINCE WE ARE DEALING WITH A CONTINUUM.

The face remains stiff and ridged with tension. Now the ears are pressed down and back, to protect them if there is a fight; the tail may still be tucked between the legs or it might be held rigidly aloft as the dog prepares to fight. Repeated nose licking and drooling are other important indicators of medium to extreme anxiety.

The eyes continue to bulge and the whites become more visible – the 'whale eye' is unmistakable. Legs are rigidly braced. In fact, the entire body may be held rigidly still for a moment – which means that the dog is very likely to bite.

Typically, the dog will still have lips clamped and pulled back which develops into showing the teeth and snarling. 'The rule of thumb for mouth expressions made by dogs is simple: the more teeth and gums are visible, the more likely the dog is signalling aggression,' says Stanley Coren. He describes this display as 'very functional … because it shows the dog's weapons (teeth) and lets the viewer understand there will be negative consequences if the warning is not taken seriously.' Ignore at your peril.

As the fear increases, so does her vocalisation. Think about how your dog reacts to fireworks and thunderstorms.

You may recall that she barks, whimpers or howls when she is afraid, especially if she is trying to signal to you that she needs help. She might pace back and forth, hide under furniture or jump on you for a protective cuddle when she is extremely agitated. That's when you might notice for the first time that she is visibly shaking with fear and her heartbeat is very rapid.

Fortunately, there is plenty that you can do in this situation. Stay calm, talk gently to reassure her, and provide lots of positive reinforcement for good behaviour because she will respond to your tone. Create a safe space. She may feel more secure in a small, enclosed area like a crate or a cupboard with some blankets, toys and treats. Play calming music or white noise to drown out the frightening sounds.

Some owners use a ThunderShirt to help combat their dog's sensory sensitivity. It soothes by providing constant pressure – effectively giving them a full body hug – and is especially effective when sensory overstimulation comes from a single source such as a thunderstorm or fireworks. It works the same way as a hug, by stimulating the parasympathetic nervous system, decreasing the level of the stress hormone cortisol and effectively putting her body into 'rest mode'.

In times of stress, distraction is always a good tactic – a chew or a puzzle toy filled with treats can help distract her and even provide a positive association to counteract the negative experience.

I'M
ANGRY

THERE ARE SEVERAL WAYS THAT A DOG MAY
DISPLAY ANGER AND AGGRESSION. FORTUNATELY,
DOMESTIC DOGS HAVE BEEN BRED TO USE
PHYSICAL AGGRESSION SUCH AS BITING AS A LAST
RESORT. EVEN DOG BREEDS WITH A REPUTATION
FOR BEING MORE AGGRESSIVE WILL GIVE PLENTY
OF WARNING BEFORE THEIR ANGER/FEAR/ANXIETY
ESCALATES INTO VIOLENCE.

Dogs avoid fighting wherever possible because in the wild, even relatively minor injuries can become life-threatening: the purpose of a dog's aggressive threat signals is to avoid violence at all costs. It's important that humans learn to recognise these signals, which include a prolonged direct stare, barking, growling, snarling (showing teeth), arching the body, walking stiffly, curling the tail between the legs or raising it high with the fur fluffed out and raised hackles (see page 60). The last two have the effect of making the animal appear bigger and more threatening.

When a dog is feeling angry or aggressive, he may also hold his ears in a different position, but this varies between breeds. Some dogs hold their ears upright and forward, which makes them look more intimidating; other breeds flatten their ears against their head when they are feeling angry or afraid, which makes them look smaller or less threatening. For protection, some dogs pin their ears back against their head when they are ready to attack or defend themselves.

When a dog starts lunging toward you or another person or animal, this is a clear sign that they are ready to attack. If possible, stop or remove whatever is causing the dog to react aggressively. Stay calm, don't shout, speak softly and don't stare at the dog. Back away smoothly to give them time and space to calm down.

However, before we reach that point of no return, it's important to read the entire body language, rather than take individual signs in isolation. For example, a commonly misunderstood sign is a wagging tail, which does not always mean that a dog is friendly and approachable. Many bad dog owners use this as a way of minimising their dog's aggression: 'He's not being aggressive, look, he's wagging his tail.'

Some dog experts advise that if your dog growls at you during play (e.g., tug-of-war), you should end the session on the premise that growling should not be tolerated under any circumstances. Most dog owners can recognise that their dog's friendly growling is all part of the game and not a cause for concern. Nevertheless, don't let him win every time.

However, when you need to remove something from your dog that he shouldn't have, he may growl, but ideally will have learned as a puppy that he can't get you to back off by growling, otherwise he will grow up believing that he can assert his will using aggression. Do not let your dog win in these circumstances. If necessary, use distraction (offer another toy or food, run excitedly to the window or get someone to ring the doorbell) rather than wrestle the item away from his jaws.

DID YOU KNOW?

There is no such thing as a physical locking jaw mechanism in any breed of dog. It's a myth.

DON'T
PUSH ME

WHEN A DOG IS ON HIGH ALERT – FEELING
SURPRISED, UNEASY, INSECURE OR FEARFUL – AND
IS COMMUNICATING THAT HE DOESN'T WANT TO BE
APPROACHED, HE MAY DISPLAY CERTAIN BODY LANGUAGE
THAT INDICATES HIS MOOD. ONE SUCH CUE IS RAISED
HACKLES: BRISTLING OF THE HAIR RUNNING DOWN THE
NECK AND BACK, MAKING HIM APPEAR LARGER AND
TALLER TO REINFORCE HIS EXPRESSION OF DOMINANCE.

Raised hackles (technically called 'piloerection') on a dog typically indicate that he is feeling agitated, scared or threatened. The hackles refer to the hair that runs along the dog's spine, which can stand up or puff out when the dog is experiencing strong emotions. Piloerection is the same involuntary response that humans experience as goosebumps and the mechanism is the same: tiny muscles in the skin's hair follicles, called arrector pili muscles, pull hair upright as they contract.

Raised hackles can be difficult to interpret accurately. In some cases, they can be a sign of excitement or arousal, such as when a dog is playing or anticipating something fun, like going for a walk. However, most of the time, raised hackles are a sign of a negative or confused emotional state.

It is worth noting that, while all dogs can have raised hackles, if this display is accompanied by a stiff-legged stance, a tense upright body posture or a slow stiff-legged forward movement, this combination only appears in dominant dogs. The good news is that dominant dogs are adept at avoiding physical violence and their body language is a way to communicate this desire for a peaceful solution, so when you see a dog displaying like this you know that s/he is dominant. Although the dog is feeling uncomfortable or defensive, it isn't a foregone conclusion that the dog is about to attack because most dogs, especially dominant ones, prefer not to engage in non-aggressive ways.

> 'For a long time, people thought that this [stiff-legged] posture indicated the dog was getting ready to fight and that aggression was unavoidable. This is far from true. Dominant dogs seldom actually fight because they don't need to do so.'
>
> Stanley Coren

Dog experts often make a distinction between two specific areas on the dog's body with respect to raised hackles. For example, ethologist Karen B London has observed in some dogs, 'A thin line (at most a few inches wide) of hair all along their back to the base of the tail'. She associates this with 'a high level of confidence'. In her experience, these dogs are 'more likely to go on offense and behave in an aggressive way than other dogs'. The other area 'is a broad patch of fur (up to eight or so inches wide) across the shoulders, which does not run more than one-quarter or one-third of the way down the back'. She associates this with 'low confidence, and I often find that these dogs are somewhat fearful'. When both occur together, 'but the hair in between the two is not raised,' this indicates 'an ambivalent emotional state' which she associates with dogs who are more reactive and unpredictable in their behaviour.

If you notice that your dog's hackles are raised, it is important to treat him carefully and respectfully. Try to remain calm and avoid making sudden movements or loud noises that could startle him. If possible, remove him from the situation that is causing him to feel uncomfortable or agitated, and give him some space and time to calm down.

Other signs of agitation include:

* **DIRECT EYE CONTACT:** Dogs may stare intently at the person or animal they perceive as a threat to communicate their intention to defend themselves if necessary.

* **GROWLING OR SNARLING:** This is a clear warning sign that the dog is feeling aggressive or defensive and may bite if pushed.

* **LIFTING A LIP OR SHOWING TEETH:** Dogs may curl their lips or show their teeth as a warning signal to stay away.

Every dog is different, and some may display different signals or combinations of signals when they feel threatened. You should be familiar with your own dog's body language in a range of situations, but you can't reliably second-guess an unfamiliar dog. However, whilst remaining cautious, the most constructive response to a dog who is displaying any of the above body signals is to remember that most attacks are avoidable, giving you the motivation to de-escalate the situation rather than run away, which could trigger the dog's pursuit response (see page 116).

I'M
CONFUSED/
CONFLICTED

WHEN EXPERIENCING UNCERTAINTY OR CONFUSION, DOGS DISPLAY A RANGE OF EMOTIONAL REACTIONS THROUGH THEIR BODY LANGUAGE. CONFUSION OFTEN CAUSES ANXIETY, SO IT ISN'T SURPRISING THAT MANY OF THESE SIGNS EXPRESS BOTH.

Head cocking or tilting is probably the clearest indication of confusion in dogs. Interpreted solely as a form of communication, its cuteness undoubtedly ameliorates an owner and broadcasts attentiveness, buying a dog crucial extra time to figure out how he should respond.

Dogs also tilt their heads when their owners are upset or in distress. We readily interpret this as empathy, but it's primarily an expression of confusion. There are also more functional reasons: by tilting his head, a dog can better fine-tune his hearing to pinpoint the sound source and determine an owner's vocal tone. There's also an important visual component. Recent research suggests that it may also help him to see your mouth more clearly.

Stanley Coren conducted an online survey with 582 dog owners and found a statistically significant correlation between muzzle size and head tilting. He theorises that dogs with longer noses cock their heads more frequently than breeds with flatter faces such as Pugs, Boston Terriers and Pekingese. If you hold your fist up to your nose, you'll notice that tilting your head allows you to see someone's mouth more clearly.

Tail position is also important. A confident dominant dog holds his tail high, allowing his scent to freely broadcast his presence. A less confident dog will lower the tail and try to keep a low scent profile. If something interesting grabs his attention, his tail may move to the horizontal, but not stiffen.

This is his alert and attentive tail position. But if he meets another dog, his tail may stiffen as they size each other up and work out their respective status. In this context, it is possible to interpret the stiff tail as an expression of uncertainty, even confusion.

During classes, dog trainers remain alert to specific signs of confusion such as lip-licking, hyperactivity or refusal to engage, lying down and opting out. Confused dogs may also scan their environment, looking urgently back and forth whilst panting, with their ears back and head held low.

Yawning can also be a form of communication in dogs. If a dog yawns directly after its owner, it's a strong indication of empathy – this mirroring is associated with feelings of love and connection (see page 36-37). However, if a dog yawns a few times on its own or sneezes, he may be feeling uncertain or uncomfortable.

This could be due to the presence of a strange person or dog, changes in your behaviour, or minor stimuli nearby that you haven't even noticed. If you look hard enough, there's always a reason. By paying close attention to your dog's body language, you can identify the triggers that cause him discomfort or anxiety and take steps to mitigate them.

I'M
BORED

A BORED DOG IS EASY TO SPOT: HE USUALLY DESTROYS YOUR BELONGINGS, MAKES A MESS AND ENGAGES IN COMPULSIVE BEHAVIOURS SUCH AS EXCESSIVE BARKING, CHEWING, DIGGING, PACING OR CONSTANTLY FOLLOWING YOU AROUND.

If your dog chews up your sofa or eats your favourite shoes, or if you're constantly picking up masticated fragments inside and outside the home (crisp packets, sticks, stuffing from his bedding and whatever else he can tear apart to pass the time), don't punish him. Instead, reward him with more of your time and attention.

Consistency is key to a dog's well-being, which is why it can be detrimental when he spends his day waiting idly for moments of excitement, uncertain whether any fun will come his way. While we readily establish a regular feeding routine for our furry friends, it's crucial to recognize that both mental and physical stimulation are not mere luxuries but daily essentials. Neglecting to fulfil these needs can have a negative impact on a dog's overall health and happiness.

You don't need to read a load of books or even use much imagination to provide your dog with ample stimulation, but you must regularly and consistently engage with them to prevent boredom and uncertainty setting in. Some people do this naturally because they love spending time with their dogs. However, even during the busiest moments in your life, you must ensure your dog's needs are still met. While it's acceptable to have an occasional frenetic day when he receives little attention, it's critical to establish firm rules and self-discipline to prevent this from becoming the standard. Feeling guilty is no substitute for ensuring that you prioritize your dog's needs.

Dr Helen Whiteside, chief scientific officer at the charity Guide Dogs, says: 'It's an outdated viewpoint to think that dogs just need a walk or two a day to be content. Without different forms of mental stimulation, dogs can begin to show signs of behavioural issues, such as anxiety and frustration, which can have a huge impact on their mental well-being.'

There are lots of ways to stimulate your dog's brain, including playing, learning, problem-solving (hiding toys or treats), obedience training for safety and learning new tricks. Varied and interesting walks also offer opportunities for your dog to engage with humans, other dogs and their surroundings. Dogs experience intense emotions such as excitement, fear and anger, and their neural chemistry is comparable to our own. What sets them apart is that they truly live in the moment rather than overthink things like humans do.

The well-being of your dog reflects your own connection to the world. Exceptional dog owners lead active lives, whilst forging meaningful emotional ties with other people, animals and the natural world. Hence, if your dog appears bored or lacks stimulation, it's vital to acknowledge that you've allowed it to happen. It cannot be stressed enough that the richness of your dog's life is your responsibility, regardless of your busy schedule. Playing more with your dog will also benefit you, so it's a double win.

I'M
DEPRESSED

DEPRESSION SYMPTOMS IN DOGS ARE VERY SIMILAR TO THOSE IN PEOPLE. A DEPRESSED DOG WILL BECOME WITHDRAWN AND LETHARGIC, WITH REDUCED ENERGY LEVELS, LOSS OF APPETITE OR INTEREST IN FOOD, FAVOURITE ACTIVITIES OR TOYS. YOU MAY NOTICE CHANGES TO THEIR SLEEP PATTERNS AND WITHDRAWAL FROM SOCIAL INTERACTIONS WITH PEOPLE OR OTHER PETS, ACCOMPANIED BY EXCESSIVE VOCALIZATION OR WHINING AND INCREASED IRRITABILITY OR AGGRESSION.

'Dog depression is a real and complex condition that can have serious impacts on a dog's emotional and physical well-being. It's important for pet owners to recognize the signs and seek professional help to provide the support and care their furry companions need.'

Dr Sarah Johnson, Canine Behaviour Specialist.

In fact, a recent survey of an admittedly small sample of one thousand dogs conducted in the UK by the charity Guide Dogs, reported that nearly three-quarters were showing signs of poor mental health. This doesn't mean that you should catastrophise every manifestation of 'the mournful eyes, the loud sigh. Our projections onto animals are often impoverished – or entirely off the mark,' warns Alexandra Horowitz in *Inside of a Dog*. Some dog breeds have a knack for looking thoroughly sulky and miserable and making us feel inexplicably guilty.But if you do have any doubts about the richness of your dog's daily life, give him more of your time, because his well-being is your responsibility.

Depression in dogs is linked to the same chemical deficiencies in the brain as in humans, including a lack of the neurotransmitter serotonin. Environmental conditions such as bereavement or separation, moving house, a new baby or pet, trauma from illness, injury or abuse such as violence or long periods of isolation, can all cause depression in dogs. The two most common triggers are the loss of a companion animal or the loss of an owner.

Unsurprisingly, in response to the scientific community's belated recognition of the emotional lives of our beloved pets, medicating dogs for depression has become big business. Some large pharmaceutical companies have even established their own pet division which earns the company over a billion dollars each year. Anti-depressants for dogs and cats are a lucrative growing part of this revenue.

However, if your dog is exhibiting the symptoms of depression, once a vet has ruled out a medical cause, there are lots of social interventions which you can use before resorting to medication. The key is early diagnosis: the quicker you identify that there is a problem, the shorter the opportunity for it to become entrenched.

Fortunately, as with humans, certain behavioural treatments such as increased exercise, play and social interaction are very effective to combat depression. You might also consider adding another dog to your family to increase social support and companionship. It isn't rocket science: John Ciribassi, past president of the American Veterinary Society of Animal Behaviour advises: 'Keep them engaged, do more of the things they like to do, get them a little more exercise, and they should be fine.'

I'M REALLY SORRY

(BUT I DON'T FEEL GUILTY)

DOGS ARE EXPERTS AT APOLOGIZING – OR AT
LEAST, GIVING THE APPEARANCE THAT THEY FEEL
SORRY – EVEN THOUGH MOST OF THE TIME THEY
PROBABLY DON'T KNOW WHY THEIR OWNER IS
RANTING AND SWEARING AND WAVING AROUND
SOMETHING THAT APPEARS TO HAVE BEEN
RECENTLY CHEWED TO PIECES.
HMMM ... CURIOUS.

One of the common ways your dog will say sorry is by making 'puppy eyes' (looking up at you whilst keeping his head lowered). He doesn't know that this makes him look super cute. He's just lowering his body and making himself appear smaller and less of a threat. He may also narrow his eyes and blink more frequently, as his anxiety increases. He will also tuck his tail between his legs whilst wagging in quick time. He might raise his paw in appeasement or flick out his tongue nervously. He may also pull back and flattens his ears and avoid eye contact, whilst remaining hyper-vigilant as he watches for your reaction.

This begs the question, 'Do dogs feel guilt?' Much though we would like to think that our dogs have developed this complex emotional response, the short answer is 'no'. In her book, *The Secret Language of Dogs*, Victoria Stilwell is unequivocal: 'Scientists believe that these submissive signals are not guilt at all but a dog's way of appeasing a person's anger even if the dog has no idea what he has done and why the person is angry.'

Dogs don't feel guilty about their actions because they don't have an internalized conscience that tells them when they have violated a social norm; instead, they rely on signals from their owners to know when they're in the doghouse.

In his book *Do Dogs Dream?*, Stanley Coren reminds us that dogs have not developed the full emotional range of humans: 'Just like a two-year-old child, our dogs clearly

73

have emotions, but many
fewer kinds of emotions than
found in adult humans.' At
birth, a human baby has
one emotion – excitement.
This quickly divides into
contentment and distress,
followed a few months later
by disgust, fear and anger, then
joy, shyness and suspicion and
finally, at about nine months of age, love. This
is as far as a dog's emotions get.

Depending on the rate of maturation of the
breed, 'dogs go through their developmental
stages much more quickly than humans do and have all of
the emotional range that they will ever achieve by the time
they are four to six months of age.'

So, it's not surprising that we refer to the innocence and
carefree nature of infants and dogs, because in humans,
shame and pride don't develop until about three years of
age and contempt takes another whole year to spoil the
party. By contrast, a dog's emotional palette stops at love;
he cannot feel shame, pride or contempt. When did a dog
ever show remorse or regret, appear arrogant or spiteful,
try to insult or belittle? Never. A dog is no more capable of
expressing these behaviours as he is to compose a sonnet
or invent gunpowder.

The closest a dog comes to spite, for example, is when he displays jealous-like behaviours, but according to dog behaviourist Nick Jones: 'dogs can be jealous over a number of things, but a more common and collective term for this would be resource guarding. This in essence is the desire to keep something for itself, such as a bone, a bed, a toy, the owner – the list is long.' Despite all this, according to Brian Hare and Vanessa Woods, co-authors of *The Genius of Dogs*: 'More than 75 percent of owners believe their dog feels guilty for disobeying. The way dogs cower and slink away when you catch them doing wrong certainly gives a good impression of guilt.' However, Alexandra Horowitz, author of *Inside of a Dog* has conducted experiments in which dogs were told by their owners not to eat a treat, then they were left alone. When the owners returned, an observer who had been watching a video camera, told the owners whether the dog had obeyed. Regardless of whether this information was accurate, Horowitz reports that the dogs appeared more guilty when they were scolded, regardless of whether they had eaten the treat: 'Being scolded despite resisting the disallowed treat, led to an extra-guilty look. This indicates that the dog has associated the owner, not the act, with the imminent reprimand.'

When your dog hears you ranting that someone has destroyed one of your trainers and then you storm into the room to confront him, he knows that he'd better get busy with submissive body language. All he wants to do is to avoid punishment because he has learned that bad things happen when he breaks human rules, no matter how arbitrary. After all, he can't tell the difference between chewing a smelly old slipper or a brand new pair of Jimmy Choos. It's all the same to him, but confusingly, your reaction is different the second time! This doesn't mean that he is being cynically manipulative. He wants to please and being scolded makes him feel anxious, so as Jennifer Arnold advises in her book, *Through a Dog's Eyes*: 'Accept his apology; it is being sincerely offered.'

I'M TOO
HOT

DOGS CAN EASILY OVERHEAT AND EXPERIENCE A FATAL HEATSTROKE WITHIN MINUTES. UNLIKE HUMANS, WHO CAN COOL DOWN BY SWEATING THROUGH THEIR ENTIRE SURFACE AREA (THEIR SKIN), THE ONLY WAY DOGS CAN CONTROL THEIR BODY TEMPERATURE IS BY PANTING TO EXCHANGE HOT AIR FOR COOLER AIR (THE FASTER HE PANTS, THE QUICKER THE HEAT LOSS) AND BY RELEASING HEAT THROUGH THEIR NOSE AND PAW PADS. ON TOP OF THIS, MANY BREEDS WEAR THICK FURRY COATS ALL YEAR ROUND, MAKING THEM MORE SUSCEPTIBLE TO DIFFICULTIES DURING WARMER MONTHS.

'Once a dog shows signs of heatstroke the damage is often already done, which is why it's so important to prevent it.'

The Blue Cross

Short-nosed dogs, puppies, elderly and overweight dogs and those with heavy coats (such as Huskies or Newfoundlands) are at the highest risk of overheating. A dog's normal body temperature ranges from 101 to 102.5°F (38.3–39.17°C). The normal body temperature for a human is generally considered to be around 98.6°F (37°C). Once a dog's body temperature exceeds 103°F, it can begin to experience heat exhaustion or heat stroke. There are several signs that your dog may be too hot and in need of rapid intervention or even veterinary attention. Some of the most common include:

* HEAVY PANTING: Dogs naturally pant to cool themselves down, but if your dog is panting heavily and continuously, it may be a sign that he is struggling to regulate his body temperature. After a lot of panting, your dog's tongue may become spatula-like, or curled into a spoon shape. This is a serious warning sign. Examine your dog's gums. If they are bright red or very pale, it may be a sign that he is overheating, and his body is struggling to circulate enough oxygen.

- **CHECK HIS HEARTBEAT:** rapid pulse can indicate that your dog is struggling to cool down and his body is working hard to maintain a normal temperature. When a dog is overheating, excessive drooling is another way that his body tries to cool him down. The drool drips onto the fur and then evaporates, which produces a small amount of cooling.

- **LETHARGY** or appearing uninterested in his surroundings is another warning sign.

- **IF YOUR DOG VOMITS OR HAS DIARRHOEA**, this is a serious indication of heatstroke, so you must cool him down immediately and seek urgent veterinary treatment.

If you suspect that your dog is too hot, it's important to take immediate action. If possible, move him to a cooler area, and offer him plenty of cool (not freezing) water. It's inadvisable to spray a hot dog with cold water (such as with a garden hose) as the sudden drop in body temperature can send him into shock. Instead, mist him with cool water and use a fan if one is available. You can also use a wet towel to soak him, especially his chest and his undercarriage. The water evaporates to produce cooling.

If your dog is exhibiting any of the above signs, contact your veterinarian straight away for further advice and treatment.

'Dogs with shorter noses, such as bulldogs and pugs (brachycephalic skulls) etc., will commonly suffer in the heat due to their anatomy hindering their breathing; this will consequently affect their ability to cool themselves down, whereas longer-muzzled dogs will cope better.'

Nigel Reed, *The Dog Guardian*

In hot weather, restrict walks to the coolest parts of the day in the morning and evening. When it's very hot, stick to mornings only as by the evening, pavements and other walking surfaces can have collected enough heat to burn his paws. Ensure that he remains hydrated by always providing access to fresh water, in a large wide bowl filled to the brim. When walking or driving with your dog, always bring a large bottle of cold water and offer him frequent drinks in a bowl. If you notice any of the above symptoms during a walk, find a shady area for your dog to rest and rehydrate.

Regardless of the temperature, under no circumstances should you leave your dog or any other pet unattended in a car, not even for a moment with the windows open. When it is a mere 22°C outside, your dog can fatally overheat in as little as ten minutes and the temperature inside a car can reach an unbearable 47°C within less than an hour.

I'M
COLD

WHEN DOGS ARE COLD, THEY MAY SHIVER,
CURL UP INTO A BALL, SEEK OUT WARM SPOTS,
OR TRY TO BURROW UNDER BLANKETS OR
OTHER COSY MATERIALS TO KEEP THEMSELVES
WARM. IT'S IMPORTANT TO KEEP YOUR DOG
WARM AND COMFORTABLE DURING COLD
WEATHER, AS PROLONGED EXPOSURE TO COLD
TEMPERATURES CAN BE DANGEROUS AND LEAD
TO HYPOTHERMIA OR OTHER HEALTH PROBLEMS.

Senior dogs, small dogs and those with short coats are more susceptible to the cold than younger, larger breeds or those with thicker fur. Signs that your dog is too cold include shaking or shivering, a hunched posture with a tucked tail, whining or barking, being anxious or uncomfortable for no other reason. Be aware of them wanting to go inside or seek shelter and if he keeps lifting his paws off the frozen ground during outside time.

Even if the winters are mild where you live, look out for signs that your dog is chilly – even though most dogs have fur coats, they like to keep toasty warm. Every dog needs a warm and comfortable place to sleep, such as a bed with blankets or a heated pad. Your dog will sleep on a bare floor if there is no other alternative, but even though he won't complain he can still feel a lot of discomfort. Don't take your lead from him. Dogs will tolerate a lot of substandard treatment from humans. Take the initiative and make sure that you treat him like a king (rather than ... well, like a dog).

When your dog sleeps on his side, it means he feels relaxed and safe and is at a comfortable temperature. This is also the position that will allow him to get the deepest sleep. Jen Jones, a professional dog trainer, behaviourist and founder of yourdogadvisor.com, says 'This position is also where you'll often notice "sleep running"and twitching during your dog's dreams, as their paws are loose and free to move'.

The lion's pose sleeping position – head on top of paws like a lion, front paws tucked in and back legs to one side – is more for rest than prolonged sleep and allows him to jump into action if required. This also indicates a comfortable temperature, but if he sleeps curled up in a ball with his legs and tail tucked underneath his body, he's too cold and trying to conserve heat. If the temperature is warm, then it's a sign that he's feeling anxious. Nervous dogs also tend to burrow underneath their blankets for security, rather than to keep warm. The most satisfying sleeping position for an owner to observe is when your dog is lying on his back with his belly showing and his legs in the air. This means he's totally content and secure and the temperature is nearly perfect (although he still might be trying to cool down).

DID YOU KNOW?

Siberian huskies are capable of working in temperatures as low as minus 75°F. They have almond-shaped eyes to keep out the snow.

I'M IN PAIN /
FEELING ILL

IF YOU SUSPECT THAT YOUR DOG IS IN PAIN OR
EXPERIENCING ANY OF THE SYMPTOMS LISTED BELOW,
IT IS IMPORTANT TO SEEK VETERINARY CARE AS SOON
AS POSSIBLE. EARLY DETECTION AND TREATMENT CAN
OFTEN PREVENT MORE SERIOUS HEALTH PROBLEMS
FROM DEVELOPING AND CAN HELP YOUR DOG RECOVER
MORE QUICKLY. ADDITIONALLY, IT IS ALWAYS BETTER TO
ERR ON THE SIDE OF CAUTION AND SEEK PROFESSIONAL
ADVICE FROM YOUR VETERINARIAN IF YOU HAVE ANY
CONCERNS ABOUT YOUR DOG'S HEALTH.

Your dog may be living with pain without your knowledge because in the wild, any show of weakness makes an animal vulnerable to predators. Even though the pain threshold of dogs is relatively low, the inherited instinct to keep pain hidden is still strong, so it's important for you to remain vigilant with your dog. 'Canines have inherited an instinct to hide any pain that is caused by injury or infirmity,' says Stanley Coren in *Do Dogs Dream?*. 'They hide their pain . . . but unfortunately this instinctive behaviour makes it difficult for we humans to recognise when our dogs are hurting.' Sometimes an illness and even the source of the pain is obvious because your dog is limping or excessively licking/ scratching/biting an affected area and she is whimpering, whining or yelping. If none of these apply, you will have to rely on other cues such as general lethargy, disinterest in going out, withdrawal and lack of interaction, loss of appetite, drinking more or less water than usual, grumpiness and increased aggression.

You may notice a change in your dog's posture or movement. If she has flattened ears, holds her head and body low, her tail is down and she generally looks a sorry sight, seek veterinary advice. Older dogs commonly suffer from stiff joints and arthritic symptoms and may have difficulty getting up or down from a lying position, or to walk upright on a wooden or tiled surface. If she has trouble getting up or down stairs (struggles to climb up, loses control and slides down several steps), this is also a sign of weakness and possible illness, so it's safest to get her checked out.

85

These are the top 16 signs that your dog may be ill.

1. Bad breath, panting or drooling.
2. Excessive drinking or urination.
3. Appetite change – unexplained weight loss or gain.
4. General lethargy, reduction in energy/activity level, lack of interest.
5. Sleeping more than usual.
6. Lameness or stiffness.
7. Coughing, sneezing, laboured breathing.
8. Skin complaints, hair loss, sores, lumps.
9. Frequent vomiting or change in bowel movements.
10. Dry, red, or cloudy eyes.
11. Runny eyes or nose.
12. Black stool, contains blood or mucus.
13. Difficulty urinating or defecating.
14. Shaking of the head.
15. Excessive licking.
16. Red or swollen gums.

The symptoms mentioned above indicate an underlying illness. However, it's important to recognize the signs of medical emergencies, such as snake bites, poisoning and other critical conditions.

SNAKE BITES If your dog doesn't yelp in pain, you may only suspect she's been bitten when she becomes agitated and restless, and begins panting and drooling excessively. You may then be able to locate the bite through signs such as redness, bleeding or swelling. If you spot a snake nearby, take a photograph if possible or examine it from a safe distance so that you can describe its appearance to your vet. This will help them to administer the appropriate anti-venom. If the snake is venomous, your dog may experience vomiting, diarrhoea, shock, collapse, seizures and even paralysis. The quicker you can get her treated, the better her chances of making a full recovery.

BEE OR WASP STINGS can cause localized irritation and swelling, which typically subsides within a few hours. When a bee stings, its barbed sting may lodge in the skin and must be removed to prevent infection. Wasps, being capable of multiple stings, can pose a greater risk. It's important to look out for signs of an allergic reaction, such as swelling around the mouth, throat, neck, or head, difficulty breathing, weakness or collapse. If any of these symptoms occur, seek veterinary assistance immediately.

POISONING: Dozens of house and garden plants are poisonous to dogs, as well as many foods and other items common around the home. These include (but are not limited to) chocolate, grapes, raisins, onions, garlic, chives, alcohol, coffee beans, blue cheese, macadamia nuts, walnuts, pistachios, pecans, Persin (a fungicidal toxin present in the avocado), Xylitol (an artificial sweetener found in sugar-free gum and many other products), raw or undercooked meat, Niger seeds for birds, slug pellets, Vitamin D tablets, human drugs and anything mouldy (keep your dog away from food waste).

The symptoms of poisoning can vary depending on the type and amount of the poisonous substance ingested. These symptoms may include agitation, drooling, panting, nausea, vomiting, diarrhoea, oral irritation, pale gums, heart issues, excessive bruising or bleeding, unsteadiness on feet, drowsiness, breathing problems, tremors and convulsions. If you suspect that your dog has ingested something toxic, it's crucial to seek immediate veterinary treatment.

YOU'RE
THE ALPHA HERE

DOGS EXHIBIT TWO TYPES OF SUBMISSIVE BODY LANGUAGE: ACTIVE AND PASSIVE. IN BOTH CASES, THE DOG WILL MAKE HERSELF APPEAR SMALLER AND LESS OF A THREAT BY LOWERING HERSELF TO THE GROUND. SHE MAY LIE FLAT WITH EVEN HER HEAD ON THE GROUND OR LIE ON HER BACK EXPOSING HER TUMMY, WITH EARS FLATTENED AND HER TAIL TUCKED BETWEEN HER LEGS OR WAGGING LOW AND FROM SIDE TO SIDE.

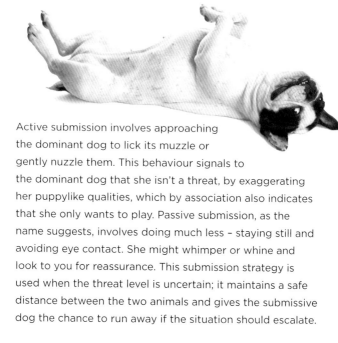

Active submission involves approaching the dominant dog to lick its muzzle or gently nuzzle them. This behaviour signals to the dominant dog that she isn't a threat, by exaggerating her puppylike qualities, which by association also indicates that she only wants to play. Passive submission, as the name suggests, involves doing much less – staying still and avoiding eye contact. She might whimper or whine and look to you for reassurance. This submission strategy is used when the threat level is uncertain; it maintains a safe distance between the two animals and gives the submissive dog the chance to run away if the situation should escalate.

If your dog is acting submissively, she may yet change her posture and adopt more aggressive body language if she feels cornered or if the other dog doesn't respond favourably to her submissive displays.

Some dogs, especially puppies, experience submissive urination, either deliberately to show deference or by accident through fear. Don't scold or punish your dog as this will only make the issue worse and many puppies grow out of this behaviour on their own anyway.

Some dogs smile or grin with their teeth exposed when they are feeling anxious and submissive. This is not the same as baring the teeth, which is an overtly aggressive act. Smiling when feeling uncomfortable in the presence of strangers is meant to convey friendliness and approachability, just as it does in many Western human cultures.

Licking lips is another common appeasement gesture intended to send a calming, non-threatening message and is sometimes done to signal submission to people or other animals, most often when the dog is anxious or afraid.

Sometimes, even dogs that are generally submissive may exhibit dominant behaviours under certain conditions. For example, a dog that is usually friendly and playful with other dogs in public may display dominant body language when other dogs visit their home. In this situation, the owner should reassure their dog that the visitors are welcome and not a threat.

If this develops into a persistent problem and your dog becomes uncharacteristically aggressive or agitated in the presence of visitors, introduce them gradually and reward her with lots of praise and other rewards. Reward her when she is being calm, not in an attempt to calm her down while she is being aggressive, otherwise she will associate rewards with being aggressive. Don't lose sight of the goal of teaching your dog that welcoming guests is a pleasant and rewarding experience.

If a strange dog shows submissive behaviour towards you, it could indicate that she views you as dominant or possibly even a threat, so don't do anything that could make her feel more anxious or she might resort to defensive aggression. Stay calm, friendly and relaxed and don't do anything to assert your dominance. She has already acknowledged that you're the boss, so wear your status with equanimity. Don't stare at her or do anything else that might ramp up her stress levels.

Gift-giving is a completely natural behaviour for dogs and many breeds do this. When your dog brings you one of her toys, it could be an invitation to play (the gift is her tug-of-war rope or a ball), a way of welcoming you home (rushing off to find a toy helps to dissipate some of her excitement) or it could simply be an unsolicited gift, which is a submissive gesture and healthy sign of affection and trust.

It may not always be convenient to drop everything and rough house with your dog every time you come home but do make a point of giving her lots of fuss and praise for her gift-giving. It builds trust and gives her the satisfaction of knowing that her efforts to communicate have been successful.

DID YOU KNOW?

After eating her dinner, if your dog immediately seeks you out, it means that you are her next favourite thing after food!

EXCUSE ME,
I'M THE ALPHA HERE

HIERARCHY AND DOMINANCE ARE IMPORTANT IN CANINE SOCIAL RELATIONSHIPS, BUT A LOT OF MISINFORMATION STILL SURROUNDS THIS ISSUE. WHEN TWO OR MORE DOGS MEET FOR THE FIRST TIME, THEY WILL USE DOMINANT AND SUBMISSIVE BEHAVIOUR TO QUICKLY ESTABLISH A SOCIAL ORDER. THIS IS NORMAL, NATURAL AND DESIRABLE.

In a pack, each dog has a specific social ranking or position, but this can still be impacted by changes in the group's composition, individual behaviours and social dynamics. Interestingly, it doesn't necessarily equate to physical dominance. 'Leaders in a feral dog pack are not the most physically dominant individuals. Instead, dogs with the strongest affiliative bonds or friendships in the group are the most likely to be the leaders,' explain Brian Hare and Vanessa Woods in their book, *The Genius of Dogs*. In other words, the social hierarchy of dogs has more in common with politics than cage fighting.

'For dogs, a healthy social order avoids conflict and is flexible, depending on what matters to each dog,' explains Victoria Stilwell in *The Secret Language of Dogs*. 'Rather than increasing aggression, dominant behaviour evolved as a way to actively avoid it … Unlike humans in their dominant behaviour over dogs, which can be physically violent, a truly dominant dog might exert his dominance by using non-violent behaviour to defuse a situation.' This may involve a gesture as subtle as 'a simple look, a paw touch or a head draped over the shoulders of another dog'.

Humans do well to appreciate this subtlety instead of adopting the now widely discredited practice of dominating and training dogs by using physical punishment of any sort, or through psychological intimidation. Like children, dogs learn best through, humane, fear-free positive techniques that build trust and confidence. The human need to physically dominate stems from the misguided belief that all dogs want to be the Alpha in the household and that they need 'taming'. In fact, the opposite is true. Dogs don't want that responsibility – it's too stressful. Plus, they're already domesticated, they aren't feral.

When two dogs meet, they communicate their social status through body language. The dominant dog may assume a stiff-legged upright stance, and if the other dog accepts this, it may break eye contact and either lie down or perform a play bow to express submission. A dominant dog will often hold direct eye contact with other dogs or people as a way of asserting his authority.

Dogs may use vocalization such as growling or snarling to assert their dominance when they feel challenged. Even this apparent standoff rarely escalates into violence, unless an owner steps in aggressively, or if one of the dogs has underlying psychological issues (e.g., has suffered a dog attack as a puppy or been mistreated).

After a broad hierarchy has been established, the dogs will sniff each other's faces, mouths, necks and hindquarters to gain further information, including social ranking, gender, reproductive status, age, health and emotional state.

If the dogs have a similar status, they may stand flank to flank, both sniffing each other's hindquarters while standing stiffly. However, if one of the dogs braces its feet and extends its head with its ears erect, it indicates that the hierarchy has not been established and the dog is ready to fight for dominance. In practice, there won't be a fight; one of the animals will back down to protect both from potential injury.

The tail position of a dominant dog is unmistakable: when a dog holds its tail high with a slight curl over the hindquarters, it indicates confidence and dominance while also allowing its scent to spread confidently into the air to announce its presence. If the tail stiffens, especially when encountering another dog, it suggests the possibility of conflict as they evaluate each other. If the dog then raises its tail up stiffly again, it's communicating its dominance without being aggressive; it's simply asserting itself.

Dogs often demonstrate their dominance by placing their head or paw on another dog or by shoulder-barging them. Leaning on another dog is also a less aggressive form of shoulder-barging. Sometimes, your dog may even try to shoulder-barge you to get you to move from a particular spot. Even though this may seem hilarious, hold your ground (but don't shout or resort to physical punishment). Remember that you're in charge, and you can calmly sit wherever you want.

I'M AN ALPHA WANNABE

IN HER BOOK, *WHY DOES MY DOG DO THAT?*, SOPHIE COLLINS DESCRIBES A FAIRLY COMMON SOCIAL SITUATION THAT REVEALS A YOUNG TWO-YEAR-OLD BELGIAN MALINOIS TO BE WHAT SHE CALLS AN 'ALPHA WANNABE'. THE DOG'S OWNER DESCRIBES HIM AS SEEMING 'UNEASY PLAYING IN A GROUP. HE JOINS IN, BUT IF YOU WATCH HIM CLOSELY, THE ROLE THAT HE SEEMS TO TAKE UP IS MUCH MORE LIKE THAT OF A POLICEMAN OVERSEEING THE GAME THAN A PARTICIPANT.' THE DOG WILL ROUTINELY WATCH TWO OTHER DOGS PLAYING, THEN SUDDENLY 'BARGE IN AND BREAK IT UP'.

Sophie Collins explains that this behaviour is typical of
this 'young, rather anxious and status-conscious dog'.
She interprets his disruptive behaviour as being caused
by the dog's desire to be in charge, even though he lacks
the 'natural seniority, confidence and status to attract the
deference he longs for'. He breaks up the play because he
can't control it.

When 'he appoints himself bossy overseer of
the game,' Collins compares the dog to a
nervous child who starts bullying. The dog
can't relax because he is too conscious of
his own status and can't tolerate the way in
which status organically changes during normal
dog play; for example, the chaser becomes the chased and
dogs challenge each other whilst sending signals that it's all
just a game. Regardless, some dogs are too self-conscious
and take themselves a bit too seriously to let their fur down
and join in with the knockabout fun. We all know plenty of
humans who are the same.

Collins warns that alpha wannabes 'can be some of the
hardest dogs for owners to "teach" to relax'. She offers a
solution: the owner needs to step in, take charge and stop the
unwanted policeman behaviour by providing a distraction,
such as lining all the dogs up to sit for a treat. In this way, all
the dogs become subordinate to the human and the nervous
dog will be relieved when the human takes charge.

The idea of an 'alpha wannabe' is becoming increasingly controversial. It is often applied to interactions between dogs, which can be unhelpful, but it should not be used to describe the relationship between a dog and a human.

We used to think that dogs form rigid hierarchies which never change but they are much more fluid and adaptable in their social interactions. The relationships they form with other dogs and humans are based on individual personalities, experiences and context, so in any group of dogs meeting

99

and playing in the park, the idea of the emergence of a 'dominant' or 'alpha' dog is misleading.

If you suspect that you have an 'alpha wannabe' dog, it's probably more helpful to think of him as anxious and insecure and to acknowledge that it's your job to make him feel more relaxed and comfortable in the presence of other dogs. Your natural instinct might be to punish this proto-dominant behaviour (especially when other dog owners are watching and judging you), but this will make the situation worse.

Socialisation takes time and practice, and requires patience and consistency on your part. Keep introducing your dog to other dogs, people and environments to help him become more confident and well-adjusted.

> 'Far too many times dog owners have been given advice to "show the dog who's boss" and "be the alpha." The unfortunate side effect of this thinking is that it creates an adversarial relationship between the owner and their dog … Such misinformation damages the owner-dog relationship, and may lead to fear, anxiety and/or aggressive behaviours from the dog.'
>
> The Association of Professional Dog Trainers

It used to be fashionable amongst certain dog trainers for the owner to assert him/herself as the Alpha in the household, for fear that otherwise, chaos would ensue. Fortunately, this potentially very damaging attitude towards caring for dogs has been debunked, along with cruel training techniques such as alpha rolls, scruff shakes and 'pack rules'. These included such behaviours as always eating before your dog, not allowing a dog to be higher up than you (i.e., no sofas or beds), walking through doorways before your dog, not letting your dog walk ahead of you, etc. If you have always suspected that this exhausting and pointless posturing takes all the fun out of having a dog and reveals more about the insecurities and power complex of its human proponents, then pat yourself on the back – you can feel vindicated.

This mistaken belief system arose from the misguided belief that dogs and wolves are close cousins, when they are as different as we are to great apes. This misapprehension arose mainly because of overreliance on the study of wolves in captivity rather than in the wild. Also, there is no need for humans to impose power hierarchies on dogs.

Veterinary behaviourist, Dr Amy Pike and licensed veterinary technician Jessey Scheip explain in an article for *Veterinary Practice News*: 'No species in the animal kingdom creates dominance hierarchies with another species. When it comes to a dog's response to its humans, dogs naturally defer to our wishes. If an owner believes a dog isn't listening and following instructions, they should consider possible reasons why and remove the idea of a "dominant dog" from the list.'

WOOF, WOOF, GROWL

DOGS HAVE A REPERTOIRE OF GROWLS AND BARKS, WHINES AND HOWLS, GROANS AND SIGHS, SO IT MAKES SENSE TO DEAL WITH THEM ALL AT THE SAME TIME. WOLVES ARE NOT KNOWN TO BARK EXCEPT WHEN THEY ARE YOUNG AND EXCITED. THIS IMPLIES THAT IN THE PAST, THE EARLIEST DOG OWNERS LIKELY BRED THEIR NOISIEST CANINES TOGETHER INTENTIONALLY TO PRODUCE HIGHLY VOCAL DOGS THAT WOULD INSTINCTIVELY BARK WHENEVER OUTSIDERS APPROACHED.

If puppies are given the opportunity to remain with their mothers and littermates for a minimum of eight weeks, they will learn the fundamental canine signals. These signals are comprised of three components: the tone, length, and repetition of a sound. Dogs utilize low-pitched sounds like growls to communicate aggression or danger, whereas they employ high-pitched sounds like yelps and squeals to demonstrate friendliness, fear, or pain and avoid confrontation. The use of pitch is not limited to dogs, as it is widespread among many birds and mammals.

The second component of canine signals pertains to the duration of the sound. As per the general principle, shorter sounds are typically associated with pain, fear, or an urgent need. In *How to Speak Dog*, Stanley Coren suggests that 'The longer the sound, the more likely that the dog is making a conscious decision about the nature of the signal and the behaviours that are about to follow'. Therefore, a dominant dog's threatening growl, indicating that it means business and is not bluffing, will be both low-pitched and 'long and sustained'. Conversely, if a dog growls using shorter bursts that are less sustained, it indicates that it is fearful and less confident about winning a fight.

The third component is the repetition rate of the sound. Coren explains: 'Sounds that are repeated often, at a fast rate, indicate a degree of excitement and urgency. Sounds that are spaced out, or not repeated, usually indicate a lower level of excitement or a passing state of mind.'

103

LOW GROWLS are associated with aggression and warding off threats.

HIGH GROWLS: the higher the pitch of a growl, the less threatening it is perceived to be. High-pitched growls are typically more playful and commonly heard during activities such as tug-of-war, whereas your dog might use a low growl while you are removing something which she wants to keep, such as food or one of your best shoes, from her jaws. Some dog trainers advise that you should not tolerate your dog growling at you, even playfully, but there is a clear difference between play growling and a real warning. Most dog owners can distinguish between them. The key principle here is that of warning, which you don't want to discourage, otherwise you will leave her with no option but to escalate to a bite without growling first.

SHORT GROWLS: most dogs communicate their apprehension or uncertainty through a series of brief consecutive or intermittent growls. It's her way of evaluating the situation, so it's advisable to allow her some time to work things out.

LONG, SUSTAINED GROWL: this is more definite; your dog has made up her mind that she doesn't like something and she's letting you know. The longer the growl, the more confident she is about this potential threat.

LOTS OF VOCALIZATIONS IN A ROW: a general rule is that the more your dog repeats a sound, the more urgent the situation and the more excited she is. If she is barking excitedly and wagging her tail, it could be a sign of happiness or excitement. On the other hand, if she is growling or snarling aggressively while making repetitive vocalizations, it's a sign of fear, anxiety or aggression. Therefore, it's crucial to observe her body language and the context to interpret the meaning behind these repeated vocalizations.

HIGH-PITCHED BARK: usually means 'I'm happy to see you!' or 'I'm excited to play!' or 'You've picked up my lead, so I know what's coming next!'

LOW-PITCHED BARK: 'I'm afraid of you and may fight back.'

WHINE: dogs never vocalise without a reason. A whine is the clearest sign that she wants something urgently. It could be anything from wanting to play, to expressing her pain or discomfort, hunger or thirst, or needing to be let outside to pee. Once again, it is important to observe your dog's behaviour in context to determine the cause of their whining.

HOWL: some breeds are more prone to howling than others. Some elevate it to an art form. It's her way of communicating with other dogs, getting your attention or responding to sounds like sirens. Some dog owners report that their dogs start howling when they hear an opera singer hitting the high notes on television. If you have more than one dog, you'll already know that one howling dog often sets off the rest.

SIGHS AND GROANS, HEAVY BREATHING: dogs sigh, groan and breathe heavily to communicate their emotions in a variety of contexts. These can range fromcontentment to relaxation, stress or anxiety, boredom, frustration or restlessness, or attention-seeking. It can also be an expression of physical discomfort or pain, so once again, context is everything.

WHERE ARE YOU?
I'M LONELY

WHEN YOU HEAR THE DOG NEXT DOOR MAKING
A PROLONGED STRING OF BARKS AND/OR
HOWLS WITH MODERATE TO LONG INTERVALS
IN BETWEEN, THIS MEANS, 'IS THERE ANYONE
THERE? WHERE ARE YOU? I'M LONELY FOLKS,
ARE YOU COMING HOME SOON? PLEASE CAN YOU
LET ME OUT OF THE KITCHEN NOW?' SHE'S BEEN
LEFT ON HER OWN AND SHE DOESN'T LIKE IT.

WHAT IS MY DOG REALLY THINKING?

As a rule, if your dog appears relaxed when you are preparing to leave the house, that's a good sign. She has learned that you will eventually come back home, so although she might not be happy that you are going on a walk without her, she isn't agitated. Ifshe gets very anxious, either barking, pacing or seeking attention before you leave, and if she causes damage or a mess while you're away, she is experiencing high levels of stress when left alone.

Some people still believe dogs develop separation anxiety because they have been allowed to believe that they are the Alpha in the household and that they subsequently feel overwhelmed by the responsibility of worrying about their absent human family. This is a myth, which is debunked on page 94.

It's common for dogs to get anxious or agitated when they sense that their care givers are about to leave the house. This is because they are sociable animals that need company and stimulation. Here are some tips to help prevent or reduce your dog's anxiety before you leave:

- Practice desensitisation: gradually expose your dog to the stimuli that trigger their anxiety, such as putting on your shoes or picking up your keys, in a non-threatening way. This will help your dog learn to associate these actions with positive experiences, rather than with anxiety and stress.

- Leave the house for very short periods of time and reward your dog for calm behaviour before you leave. Gradually increase the time you are away, so that she learns that you will always return home.

- Try to keep your departures and arrivals as calm and low-key as possible. Avoid making a big fuss over your dog before you leave and when you return, as this can reinforce her anxiety. Your dog will, quite logically, wonder why you are being so reassuring when you leave if it's no big deal. By doing this, you are providing the cue that she has something to fret about.

- Use positive reinforcement: give her treats, praise, or affection when she is relaxed, rather than anxious.

- Do not punish her if she has 'misbehaved' in any way while you were out, otherwise you will increase her anxiety and merely reinforce the undesirable behaviour.

Dogs are social animals and crave attention and stimulation, so it's important to provide them with activities and toys to keep them happy and engaged while you're out. Here are some ways to keep your dog happy while you're away:

- Provide toys and treats to keep her mentally stimulated and entertained. These may include puzzle toys, treat-dispensing or chew toys. Many owners swear by a Kong chew filled with peanut butter.

- Leave the TV or radio on to provide calming music or background noise. This can help her feel less alone while you're out, but only do this if she responds favourably. Sometimes the noise can overstimulate your dog, especially if a dog barks on the television. Also, dogs have blue-yellow dichromatic vision, so colourful cartoons can be confusing. 'Some dogs may like to watch TV, and others completely ignore it,' says veterinarian Dr Aliya McCullough. 'It's an individual decision that pet parents can make based on their dog's preference and behaviour.'

- If you're going to be out for a long time, consider hiring a dog walker to come and take her for a walk. This will burn off some energy and encourage her to rest or sleep.

- Giving her a cosy safe space, such as her crate can help prevent destructive behaviour and promote calmness. Whenever you go out, place your dog in her crate with some toys, water and a comfortable bed and gradually increase the amount of time she spends in there. For best results, use this from early puppyhood.

- Leave her with access to a window so she can look outside and watch the world go by. This can provide entertainment and stimulation for your dog.

There are many monitor and phone app resources that can help you record your dog's barking and/or monitor her movement when you're away. Some allow you to monitor your dog using your phone's camera and microphone, and have barking detection features that record your dog's barking and send you notifications.

Others allow you to monitor and record your dog's sounds, have motion detection features that send you alerts when she moves, or let you set up 'watch and interact' functions. Do some research before setting up any monitors and apps to check you are using one that supports your dog and household appropriately.

DID YOU KNOW?

The ten dog breeds most likely to suffer from separation anxiety, in order, are Labrador Retriever, Border Collie, Cavalier King Charles Spaniel, Jack Russell Terrier, German Shepherd, Australian Shepherd, Bichon Frise, Vizsla, German Shorthaired Pointer and Toy Poodle.

OH NO, NOT CHILDREN

MANY DOGS ARE VERY PATIENT IN THE COMPANY
OF CHILDREN AND ARE SURPRISINGLY TOLERANT
OF THEIR NOISE LEVELS AND UNPREDICTABLE
ENERGY. HOWEVER, SOME DOGS UNDERSTANDABLY
BECOME ANXIOUS AROUND UNFAMILIAR CHILDREN
AND ACTIVELY AVOID THEM, HIDING BEHIND
FURNITURE OR ESCAPING INTO ANOTHER ROOM
WHENEVER THEY ARE AROUND.

If your dog responds to unfamiliar children in this way, it's no surprise, as Sophie Collins explains in her book, *Why Does My Dog Do That?*. 'Toddlers, in particular, may really frighten them. A small child doesn't respect personal space, is at face level to many dogs, and communicates in very high-pitched, unpredictable squeals and shouts ... Kids also tend to stare unblinkingly at objects of interest, which dogs may read as a challenge.' In *How to Speak Dog*, Stanley Coren describes the research of the French psychiatrist Boris Cyrulnik who analysed video footage of interactions between dogs and children. He was initially surprised to discover that dogs 'reacted more negatively and fearfully' when interacting with neurotypical children than they did when interacting with children who were neurodivergent. After hours of close observation, he concluded that the difference was connected to the children's body language and 'the signals these two groups of children were sending to the animals'.

Cyrulnik noted that the neurotypical children tended to look straight at the dogs, which in dog language is perceived as a threat. They smiled broadly: 'a big, broad, open-mouthed smile. To the animal, this means that the children have just bared their teeth' which to a dog is an act of aggression. 'Typically, the children also raised their arms high and forward toward the dogs ... the equivalent of a dog rearing up to make itself appear larger and more dominant, and threatening attack'. He also describes the children as holding out their hands with their fingers extended as they approach the dog, which Coren likens to a threatening

113

'open mouth with teeth'. Finally, the children 'usually rush directly toward the dog in a grand display of affection and enthusiasm'. Coren concludes that this is the reason that so many children are bitten each year by dogs which under normal circumstances are friendly and non-aggressive.

By contrast, Cyrulnik reported that some of the neurodivergent children in the study acted very differently: 'They avoided looking directly at the animals, so there was no initial threat. They moved more slowly and often approached at an angle to the side, instead of face-on … [keeping] their arms low,' all of which made them appear non-threatening to the dogs.

Although it is important to stress that the children in both groups were all individuals with their own unique physicality and personality, Cyrulnik nevertheless was able to identify specific body language of certain individuals within both groups that the dogs found either threatening or non-threatening. This shows that our body language is very important when we interact with dogs, especially when they are unfamiliar.

When you encounter a shy or nervous dog whose body language is expressing anxiety and fear, you should turn your head away. Don't look directly at her. Angle your body so that your side is facing the dog to make you less wide and threatening. Walk slowly and casually, approaching her obliquely rather than walking directly towards her: keep your side to her, as if you intend to walk right past her.

When you get a bit closer, squat or kneel and pretend to be interested in something on the ground – pretend she isn't your focus at all. This is a good trick to make you seem smaller and disinterested. Once you are very close, extend your arm and offer your hand with your fingers curled in and together, or with the owner's permission, hold a treat in your cupped hand. Keep avoiding direct eye contact but talk reassuringly in a gentle calm voice, using the dog's name. If you pet the dog, keep your hand low, stroking the chest first before the head. Maintain this low arm and hand postion, always below her head level to avoid sending a dominance signal which she could interpret as aggression.

When a dog is in full threat mode – mouth open with bared teeth, ears back, gums showing, hackles raised – use these same body language tricks to make your escape (don't run as this will only trigger his pursuit response). Avert your gaze, blink once or twice, and yawn as you back away slowly. Coren advises opening your mouth a little at this point, 'which indicates a bit of a counterthreat, suggesting that you will respond to any aggression if the dog initiates it'. He also recommends only turning your side to the dog when you are a good distance away. If he moves towards you, you must face him to show that you are no pushover, but then send more signals that you do not want to fight – exaggerated eye blinks, looking to the side and down, yawning, and so on, as you continue to back off.

I'M NOT SURE

ABOUT THESE HUGS AND KISSES

WE LOVE TO CUDDLE AND KISS OUR DOGS TO SHOW
OUR AFFECTION, BUT IT IS SUCH AN INGRAINED
NATURAL BEHAVIOUR FOR HUMANS THAT WE
RARELY STOP TO CONSIDER WHETHER DOGS ENJOY
OR EVEN UNDERSTAND WHAT OUR KISSES MEAN.
MOST OF US ARE DIMLY AWARE THAT DOGS AS A
SPECIES AREN'T NATURAL HUGGERS AND KISSERS
OR THAT MANY DOGS DISLIKE THEM; ALSO, ALL
THOSE KILLJOY DOG EXPERTS TELL US NOT TO, BUT
IT SEEMS WE JUST CAN'T HELP OURSELVES.

Conversely, there is lots of anecdotal evidence from thousands
of dog owners, possibly yourself included, that dogs love hugs
and kisses and they nuzzle in or actively encourage them by
jumping up for affection. So, what's the real story?

The first thing to establish is whether dogs understand
what kisses from people mean. Although dogs are experts
at reading human emotions, a puppy doesn't instinctively

117

know what kisses are. She must be taught. Certified animal behaviourist, Amy Shojai explains: 'Some dogs enjoy this, if taught what it means … [but] people kissing them could potentially send mixed signals.'

Just because we know what kisses mean, it doesn't follow that the dog will take it that way. An additional complication is that when humans kiss romantically, they stare into each other's eyes, which in dog language is usually interpreted as confrontational. Furthermore, dogs tend to approach each other sideways rather than head-on, so it can be confusing for a dog to suddenly see a human face approaching directly, with a big toothy grin (another potentially confrontational body sign for dogs). No wonder some dogs get so confused when we shower them with affection.

> 'In general, if a dog licks you, they are showing affection. However, if the dog licks someone who is agitated or excited this could be a symptom of stress. By licking that person, they are trying to relieve their stress because they know this is a welcome gesture.'
>
> Victoria Stilwell

If your dog responds to your kisses by licking you, even this response isn't clear cut. Dog licks can often be a show of affection towards humans, but not always. When a dog licks another dog's mouth it is to send the message, 'I am not a threat. You're the boss.' If your dog licks you in response to kisses, she could be trying to appease you rather than returning your kisses. Dogs don't instinctively lick to show affection, but they quickly learn that licking can get our attention, and that it often evokes a positive response.

Other appeasement behaviour includes yawning, sniffing, scratching, sneezing and lip-licking; if you see any of these in response to your hugs and kisses, then back off and give your dog some space because those signs are unequivocal. They're just not that into it.

The key is to be attentive to how your dog responds to your affection. If she likes it, she shouldn't move away or try to avoid being kissed. When you stop kissing and cuddling, if she moves closer to you, slaps her paw on the ground or makes a gesture which you recognise means 'Don't stop, more please!' then you know she's comfortable.

119

I WANT SOME OF
THAT

WHEN HE LOOKS UP AT YOU WITH THOSE BIG
PUPPY DOG EYES AND SITS SO PATIENTLY WAITING
FOR YOU TO GIVE HIM SOME SCRAPS FROM YOUR
TABLE, IT'S SO HARD TO RESIST. IT FEELS ALMOST
CRUEL TO IGNORE HIM, ESPECIALLY WHEN HE'S
BEING SO WELL-BEHAVED. HE ISN'T JUMPING UP,
HE ISN'T BARKING … BUT THOSE EYES. HE JUST
WON'T GIVE YOU A MOMENT'S PEACE. SURELY
IT WON'T HURT, JUST THIS ONCE?

Why do dogs beg? Because it works. If you respond to your dog's begging by giving him some of your food, you'd better be prepared for him to continue begging for the rest of his life. It's your choice entirely, but can you tolerate being watched by a pleading dog during every meal for the next ten years and beyond? That's more than 10,000 meals. Once you start, he won't stop begging and the chances are you won't stop giving him bits and pieces.

> 'Begging can quickly turn from a cute and amusing behaviour to a frustrating and unmanageable one.'
>
> Dr Sophia Yin

It's still your choice. You're the caregiver. But here are some factors to bear in mind: First of all, some human food is poisonous to dogs (see page 88) and most of it is unhealthy, especially the scraps that we don't mind parting with. A fatty rind of bacon, a potato chip, the end of a piece of toast – all those calories add up, especially with a smaller breed. Before long, your dog has put on weight and you decide that begging will no longer be tolerated. Too late. Only now, because he expects his begging to work, once he realises that his regular method has lost its magic, he'll escalate his attention-seeking behaviour – yipping, barking, nipping, jumping, placing his head in your lap, pawing your leg and even stealing food. It's no fun to eat every meal with a dog shut out of the room barking to be let in so that he can have some of your leftovers, like in the good times … before you became so inexplicably mean.

> 'A well trained dog will make no attempt to share your lunch. He will just make you feel so guilty that you cannot enjoy it.'
>
> Helen Thomson

So, what should you do when your dog starts begging? One of the best solutions is to redirect his interest to something else, which could even be in another room, such as a toy or a snuffle mat. Occupy him by sprinkling small treats or kibble into the mat, which the dog must then search for and extract by snuffling and digging through the fabric strips with his nose and paws.

'The bottom line is, your dog will react to the way you respond to begging. Whatever you reward, you reinforce, and if "bad" or unwanted behaviours are getting him what he wants, he will keep doing it as long as it works,' advises dog expert and journalist, Scott Morgan.

Consistency is key when it comes to training your dog not to beg. Make sure everyone in your household sticks to your rules and boundaries, and avoid giving in to begging behaviour. With time and patience, your dog should learn that begging is not acceptable and won't get him what he wants.

In their book, *Outwitting Dogs*, Terry Ryan and Kirsten Mortensen recommend making a habit of cleaning up leftovers immediately so that your dog can't steal any from tables and counter tops.

> 'Remember that food is a great reward – if your dog succeeds in swiping a sandwich off the counter even once, he'll be on the lookout for sandwich number two for the rest of his life.'
>
> Terry Ryan and Kirsten Mortensen

That is a classic example of managing a situation so that your dog can't get himself into trouble. If you leave food out, not only are you tempting him with enticing smells that our limited olfactory system can't even begin to imagine, but you also create a situation that has the potential for him to misbehave, or worse, to put himself in danger if that food is toxic to dogs.

I'LL JUST LEAVE THIS
HERE

YOUR DOG'S OLFACTORY SENSE REIGNS SUPREME, SERVING AS HIS PRIMARY MEANS OF INTERPRETING HIS ENVIRONMENT. WHILE HUNTING FOR PREY MAY NOT BE AS RELEVANT NOW THAT YOU PROVIDE ALL HIS FOOD, HIS SENSE OF SMELL ALLOWS HIM TO INTERPRET THE SOCIAL CUES LEFT BEHIND BY OTHER DOGS IN THEIR URINE AND IT'S JUST AS IMPORTANT THAT HE LEAVES HIS OWN MESSAGES, TO LET OTHER DOGS KNOW THAT HE'S BEEN IN THE AREA.

However, this is not necessarily the same as 'marking territory', which is what wolves do in the wild. According to Alexandra Horowitz, in her book *Inside of a Dog*, this myth was introduced by the early-twentieth century ethologist Konrad Lorenz. 'He formed a reasonable hypothesis: urine is the dog's colonial flag, planted where one claims ownership. But research in the fifty years since he proposed that theory has failed to bear that out as the exclusive, or even predominant, use of urine marking.'

Horowitz cites studies of free-ranging dogs in India which found that 'both sexes marked, but only 20 percent of the markings were "territorial" – on a boundary of a territory … [the] notion is also belied by the simple fact that few dogs urinate around the interior corners of the house or apartment where they live'. She interprets marking as akin to a 'community centre bulletin board' advertising for hook-ups, an analogue olfactory dating app.

'Olfactory signals are probably used so widely because they do not require intentional communication. Strong smells are inescapable, they linger, and they are easy to place in many locations. This means animals do not have to understand much about their audience; eventually their signal will be received.'

Brian Hare & Vanessa Woods,
The Genius of Dogs

Dogs possess an olfactory capability that is about a million times better than that of humans. It allows them to detect and differentiate odours with remarkable subtlety and in microscopic concentrations, which is why they appear so miraculously skilled at the wide range of tasks we set them such as finding casualties trapped underneath rubble. Even a dog's physical act of sniffing makes our mechanism appear clumsy by comparison. We breathe in and out through the same holes, but in a dog's nose, inhaled and exhaled air never mixes.

Scientists have captured the sophisticated mechanics of this air flow using specialist photography, which Alexandria Horowitz also cites: 'The sniff begins with muscles in the nostrils straining to draw a current of air into them.' As a large amount of any air-based odorant enters the nose, 'again, the nostrils quiver slightly to push the present air deeper into the nose, or off through slits in the side of the nose and backward, out the nose and out of the way. In this way, inhaled odours don't need to jostle with the air already in the nose for access to the lining.' Furthermore, the exhaled air 'helps to pull more of the new scent in, by creating a current of air over it'.

Dogs urinate on top of the scents left by other dogs, so the bulletin board analogy is very apt. Male dogs usually cock one of their hind legs to spray their urine on the base of trees, lampposts, bushes, etc. and females squat and urinate on the ground, although some lift their hind leg, like males. Both sexes may also leave a visual mark, such as scratch marks on the ground (which is why your dog may scrape the floor after urinating). These scratch marks contain further scent information secreted from glands on the pads of the paws.

Adult dogs generally need to toilet three to five times a day, and most vets will recommend a maximum of between six to eight hours between toilet visits, so bear this in mind when leaving your dog for an extended period. If you notice that your dog is urinating more frequently than normal, it isn't an emergency, but it could be a sign of a urinary tract infection, diabetes, kidney or liver disease, or incontinence. As always, visit a veterinarian as soon as possible.

NOTES

Use the space below to note any observations you've made about your dog's behaviour.